Our Alaska

Our Alaska

Personal Stories About Living in the North

Edited by Mike Doogan

Epicenter Press

EPICENTER PRESS INC. is a regional press founded in Alaska whose interests include but are not limited to the arts, history, environment, and diverse cultures and lifestyles of the North Pacific and high latitudes. We seek both the traditional and innovative in publishing nonfiction tradebooks and giftbooks featuring contemporary art and photography.

Publisher: Kent Sturgis
Editor: Mike Doogan
Proofreader: Sherrill Carlson
Text design: Kathy Doogan
Cover design: Sue Mattson

ISBN 0-945397-98-4 HB edition
ISBN 0-945397-94-1 SB edition

To order single copies of *Our Alaska*: Mail $22.95 for the HB edition (WA residents add $2.00 sales tax), or $16.95 for the SB edition (WA residents add $1.47), plus $5 for priority mail shipping to Epicenter Press, Box 82368, Kenmore, WA 98028; visit our website at www.EpicenterPress.com; or phone 800-950-6663 day or night.

Booksellers: Retail discounts are available from our distributor, Graphic Arts Center Publishing, Box 10306, Portland, OR 97210. Phone 800-452-3032.

PRINTED IN CANADA

First printing April 2001

10 9 8 7 6 5 4 3 2 1

Front cover illustration © from COLD STARRY NIGHT, *An Alaska Memoir*, written and illustrated by the late Claire Fejes, whose paintings of her adopted state assure her a place among Alaska's great artists. An immensely popular contemporary artist, Jon Van Zyle, created the back cover illustration ©, which appeared in his book *JON VAN ZYLE'S ALASKA SKETCHBOOK*. More information about Claire Fejes, Jon Van Zyle, and their books can be found at the publisher's website, www.EpicenterPress.com.

Contents

Introduction

In 1879, only a dozen years after the United States had paid Russia $7.2 million for the vast territory of Alaska, John Muir sailed north to test his theories about glaciation in a still-active laboratory. The book he wrote about that and subsequent trips, *Travels in Alaska,* is widely regarded as a nature writing classic. First published in 1915, it remains one of the most influential books ever written about Alaska, helping to shape the national idea that unsullied nature is so important that it overrides any other consideration about this place.

Muir's book is full of vivid and detailed descriptions of forests and rivers and bays and, particularly, the remnants of the great ice sheet that once covered southeastern Alaska. The overriding tone of the book is approval. "To the lover of pure wilderness," he wrote, "Alaska is one of the most wonderful countries in the world." Muir was so enthralled by what he saw, the reader can scarcely help but be enthralled, too.

This attitude, however, did not extend to the works

of others who had come north. Here is his description of the village of Wrangell:

> It was a lawless draggle of wooden huts and houses, built in crooked lines, wrangling around the boggy shore of the island for a mile or so in the general form of the letter S, without the slightest subordination to the points of the compass or to building laws of any kind. Stumps and logs, like precious monuments, adorned its two streets, each stump and log, on account of the moist climate, moss grown and tufted with grass and bushes, but muddy on the sides below the limit of the bogline. The ground in general was an oozy, mossy bog on a foundation of jagged rock, full of concealed pitholes.

To Muir, and to his readers, what was good about Alaska was what was untouched by humans.

About one hundred years later, another writer of naturalistic bent, John McPhee, arrived to chronicle the condition of Alaska. The book he published in 1977, *Coming into the Country,* was easily the most influential book written about this place in the second half of the twentieth century.

What McPhee found was, in some ways, not much different from what Muir had seen: wild rivers, empty forests, and stately, snow-capped mountains. But many more people lived in this place, and they had been busy in the intervening years. One of the differences was this: Where Muir had encountered only untouched nature and rude villages, McPhee found that the inhabitants had dared to build a city or two. One hundred years later, his attitude toward the state's largest city was not much different from Muir's toward Wrangell:

> Anchorage is sometimes excused in the name of pioneering. Build now, civilize later. But Anchorage is not a frontier town. It is virtually unrelated to its environment. It has come in on the wind, an American spore. A large cookie cutter brought down on El Paso could lift something like Anchorage into the air. Anchorage is the northern rim of Trenton, the center of Oxnard, the ocean-blind precincts of Daytona Beach. It is condensed, instant Albuquerque.

I have no idea how Wrangell residents reacted to Muir's description of their home, if indeed any of them read it. But when I first read McPhee's description of Anchorage, it pissed me off. I'm irritated anew when I read it today. I lived in Anchorage before McPhee came here to write his book, and I live here now, long after he has returned to his home in New Jersey. And I can tell you that people here have been too busy living their lives to worry about whether their city is pretty enough for a visiting writer.

Which is not the same as saying I disagree with him. I have been in a few of the cities in the world that are, by consensus, beautiful, and I can tell the difference. What irritates me, instead, is the assumption that since we live here, we are obliged to live differently from the people who live in, say, New Jersey. That since we live here, our houses should somehow blend into the landscape better than the houses of Trenton. That since we live here, we shouldn't be allowed to build a city that, like Princeton and every other city in America, is driven by economic considerations.

In thinking about this sharp difference of opinion I have with writers I admire, I have come to the conclusion that it arises from the differences in our respective experiences. Visitors compare Alaska to what they are familiar with. They see what is important here as what they don't have back home, nature that has not been tamed and fenced and posted. And they see any attempt to make this place more like the places they come from as a threat to what is important here. This is the visitor's perspective, and it is unavoidably the visiting writer's perspective as well.

Living your life in Alaska gives you an experience of the place that no visitor can acquire. As a child, you have nothing to compare it with, so you accept it for what it is. Cold and dark six months of the year? What's odd about that? Lots and lots and lots of empty space? So what? Moose in the roadways, bears on the hillsides, lights dancing in the night sky? Big deal. We accept Alaska for what it is, and we see the changes that make our lives richer and easier as progress, even if it means Alaska is somehow less natural — if that term has any meaning — than it was before.

But mostly, it is our lives that are in the forefront of our thoughts. We are concerned with our families and our communities, our joys and our sorrows, our histories and our futures. Alaska is the context for these stories, but it is not the stories themselves.

This book is a collection of those stories. They are not all the work of professional writers, but they are all the work of longtime Alaskans. Their collection between these covers is a small attempt to redress the imbalance between the Alaska imagined by people who don't live here, and the Alaska we live in every day. I do not expect it will become as popular and influential as the books written by visitors. But it's a start. And, polemics aside, it is a chance for us to tell some stories about people who make Alaska their home. Us. These are our stories.

— Mike Doogan

Charles Mason

Sherry Simpson teaches journalism at the University of Alaska Fairbanks and is the author of a book of essays about Alaska, The Way Winter Comes.

Growing Up Glacial

Sherry Simpson

For years and years, I never saw ice fall from the Mendenhall Glacier. This was something I thought I deserved after spending great chunks of my life at the glacier, staring at it, willing ice to fall.

The glacier calved all the time, of course. I simply never witnessed it. It was so unfair. I would be stooped over, peering at wildflowers or searching for garnets, and when a rumble or crack rolled across the landscape, I would snap my head up to see only waves surging away from a bobbing slab of ice, freshly liberated from its journey of a thousand years.

I took this failure personally, as if the glacier deliberately withheld what is, after all, a big reason we look at glaciers. I began to feel mocked. Once an earthquake shook Juneau as I stood on a mound a hundred yards from the glacier's rim. Vibrations shuddered through my feet, and a crack crept through the sand. "Now I've got you!" I thought, and waited eagerly for ice to peel away and crash into the lake. Nothing. An eerie calm reigned, the stillness breached only by the screech of gulls.

How could this be? Over three decades, I've hiked trails etched along adjacent mountains and looked down upon the glacier's cracked surface. I've skated, walked and skied across the frozen lake toward the face, foolishly passing warning signs. I've sat for long meditative afternoons watching the jumbled facade the way a fox waits for a rabbit to make a fatal bolt. Certainly I could pick that glacier out of a line-up of glaciers anywhere. That's how well I know the long swoop of ice spilling from the sky, the way this ancient hulk has wedged itself between mountains, grinding them bare in a slow-motion fender bender. And on a cloudy day, when that surreal blue radiates from fresh splits and crevasses — that's a color I've committed to memory, one that deserves its own Crayola. Mendenhall Blue, they'd call it.

But all those years of waiting for ice to fall showed me how many ways there are to look at a glacier, how many ways you can know it. For tourists, the Mendenhall is big enough to enthrall with its cold strangeness, its exotic and primeval appeal. Helicopters loft them to its surface, where they can tramp across the ice, Lilliputians conquering a blue Gulliver. But it's also small enough to pose prettily, to squeeze onto postcards and brochures. (Only sunny glacial portraits are published, never moody, rainy, realistic depictions.) Because this is wilderness conveniently located at the end of a paved highway, in twenty minutes, maybe fifteen, any tourist can do the glacier and ask the kind of questions that crack up the locals: How did it get so dirty? Who paints it blue? Where are the woolly mammoths?

For scientists, the Mendenhall is a cipher, an inexorable force that once boldly advanced into the valley and is now backing away from it. As a relic of the Little Ice Age, the glacier represents a constantly resolving equation of forces and factors, a minor laboratory in which the world remakes itself upon blank stone left in the wake of ice. The Mendenhall is nothing special, merely one of a herd of glaciers that descend from the Juneau Icefield.

For locals, the Mendenhall is a gigantic backdrop against which to play out the domestic transactions of ordinary life. People walk their dogs along the lakeshore. At night dating teenagers park at the visitor's center and steam up car windows doing who knows what. (As a former teenager, I'm afraid I do know what.) Walkers and runners make the glacier their turnaround point, pausing for a moment to inhale chilled air before they plod away again. People marry there, attend Easter sunrise services there, pose for Christmas pictures there. A woman who lives a few miles away has photographed the glacier from the same spot each year for the past forty years. People have died there, too, falling into crevasses or being crushed by the same kind of icefall I waited so long to see.

And there is a glacier that belongs to children alone. It is not so much a place as a time you belong to when you're of a certain age. When I was that age, my friends and I biked the mile to the glacier almost every day, a great pack of us racing each other and waving at tour buses grinding past. This was long before playgroups, safety helmets, and fears about child snatchers. This was a time when special effects meant attaching a playing card to your bike wheel because it made a cool thrumming sound in the spokes that echoed something vibrating inside you. This was a time when the world was a lot more fun.

When we arrived at the glacier, we tossed down our bikes and went wild, an invading force of miniature Visigoths storming a castle made of stone and ice. We swarmed the visitor's center, signed the guest book for the thousandth time, hogged the telescopes to search for mountain goats. We clambered across the massive sloping rocks that edge the lake, waded in shallow ponds, sifted sand for fool's gold. We dashed down paths dodging tourists, and then to show how bold and fearless we were, we leapt rock gullies and careened down dirt hills left behind by ice. The glacier was as familiar as the school playground and yet riddled with secret pleasures.

A kid who grows up glacial knows things most people don't. We regarded icebergs the way Midwest kids must study clouds. "Look, it's a swan," I'd say, pointing out a twisted bit of ice floating in the lake. "Not a swan, a Viking boat, you dope," someone would retort, and so on. We broke personal Popsicles from the glassy pieces that washed up along the gravely shores. One piece could last forever in your mouth, a shard of the past melting on your tongue and clicking against your teeth. Or you could carry a chunk home in your bike basket, bust it up to make ice cream, and slip a piece into some lemonade while you waited, listening to released air fizzing and popping as the years and decades and centuries decanted into your glass.

It was not all about ice, of course. Sockeye and coho salmon spawn in nearby creeks and ponds, every part of their death struggle on display. For years I played the junior biologist by collecting eggs and keeping them in a jar in my refrigerator for experiments. Sadly, I never once hatched my own school of salmon, but for many years my microscope lens wore the peach-colored residue of salmon eggs viewed just a little too closely.

This is a child's history, the kind I hope Juneau kids are still living, but I suspect most people who grew up in the Mendenhall Valley carry a private history of the glacier, too. My first real boyfriend told me he loved me on New Year's Day while we were hiking at the glacier. I was thirteen, and when I am an old lady I shall recall the crystalline intensity of that sunny day. Years later, college friends and I drank cheap red wine and skied across the lake, yelling and carrying on, but a tornado of green aurora rose behind the glacier and hushed our voices. Not long ago, I was in a small plane crossing the icefield on a painfully clear day when we turned onto the confluence with the Mendenhall and were caught in rowdy crosswinds. I swear to God, I thought we would crash. As the plane bucked and pitched, and the luggage in the rear slammed against the roof, and the pilot grimly clutched the yoke, I stared down at the glacier's riven surface and accepted the imminence of a spectacular death on ice. It was some time before I could regard the Mendenhall quite so fondly again.

Whenever I return to Juneau, I try to visit the glacier, but some journeys a person can never really make again, and this is one. The paths are paved and neatly marked. A rock buttress I once climbed so daringly is now grooved with a concrete ramp so people can stroll or wheel to the remodeled visitor center. Admission is three dollars a person. Everything in sight is interpreted helpfully with a sign or a brochure, which is nice when you want explanations but not so useful for discovering things on your own. It all seems tame and diminished.

Of course, the glacier is diminished, in size, in aspect, in volume. Year by year, it shrinks. In 1930, ice covered the very spot from where people snap so many pictures today. The distance from the road to the ice grows ever wider. This is the Mendenhall as metaphor, the way it changes day by day, almost imperceptibly, until one day you realize how far away it is, and how distant your youth is, too.

Recently I hiked up the East Glacier Trail for a long look across the ice. The face that once loomed in jagged spikes has somehow ablated, so that it slopes gently into the lake. Nugget Creek, which chiseled caverns into the glacier's flank, now sluices unobstructed into the lake, its roar a constant refrain. The stone abutment that barely emerged from ice now dominates the glacier's prow, gold and green with vegetation slowly reclaiming the territory. From this height, the Mendenhall Valley seems undisturbed by the subdivisions, roads and malls that march through the forest even as the glacier performs its about-face.

The glacier I knew as a child has changed radically, but what hasn't in this life? Who among us does not feel nostalgic, even a bit dotty, about some lost bit of childhood landscape — an abandoned lot next door, a scrap of woodlands, a swimming hole? Once I heard California legislator Tom Hayden talk about the importance of a folkloric landscape, of knowing a piece of ground so well that you could discuss, say, that old stubborn boulder in the north pasture.

The Mendenhall Glacier, I realized, is layered with such stories and anchored by local history. It is a place so familiar that surrounding mountains seem like cherished, elderly uncles, and the luminescent blues are as sentimentally evocative as your high school's team colors, and the feel of a pebble smoothed by ice is as soothing in the hand as a rosary bead.

For those of us who grew up with it, the glacier is a calendar, a place holder, a reminder that time scrapes against us, too. The past, I've noticed, recedes far more quickly than ice. The more I think about it, the more I recall having seen ice fall from the Mendenhall once, but if I actually did, the memory is hazy and indistinct, and perhaps constructed entirely out of desire. Anyway, the older I get, the less that drama seems necessary. As it turns out, it is the waiting that matters, not the falling.

Joanna Carlson

Dana Stabenow lives in Anchorage and is the author of sixteen novels.

A Son of Martha

Dana Stabenow

"The doctor said if he had to make a bad guess, it'd be Lou Gehrig's disease."

It was January 1998. We were sitting in Dad's living room in Airport Heights. I couldn't look away from him, I think afraid he would vanish if I did. He couldn't meet my eyes.

I never met my father until I was fourteen, as my parents split up when I was six months old. It wasn't quite a Spenard divorce — everyone lived — but they didn't speak again until I needed to go to a dentist. There wasn't one in Seldovia, so my mother called him in Anchorage and said, "Dana's coming up to get her teeth fixed, and by the way, you're paying for it." In the interim, I never got so much as a birthday card, a Christmas present, child support. I was really angry about that later on for, oh, about five minutes, but by then I'd fallen head over heels in love with him and what the hell.

The first time I saw him was when he met my airplane in Anchorage. He was six feet, four inches tall, with pale skin that went red and peeled in the sunshine, bright blue eyes, and a thick mane of white-blond hair of which he was very proud. He had big hands and a bigger voice, deep, carrying, resonant. For years my friend Kathy and I had imagined me meeting my father, and now here was this tall, handsome god claiming to be that man. That afternoon in Anchorage his pedestal was ready for mounting, it was very high, and he looked great on it.

I got my teeth fixed and went home, and we saw each other off and on after that. When I graduated from high school, and Mom and I moved to Anchorage so I could go to college, Dad bought me a car, a 1964 Ford Falcon. Like every car he ever bought in his life, it needed work, but he was a master mechanic, and he always had privileges at whatever shop he was working. We took the Falcon down there together, where he taught me how to change the oil and the spark plugs, adjust the points and do a lube job. You learn a lot about a man in spending time with him under a car. We were changing out the oil filter when he mentioned his brother Danny, and how I was supposed to have been a boy named Dan. Until then I hadn't known I'd had uncles. I inquired further and discovered that I'd had three, all dead by the time I met dad: Danny in a dynamite explosion when they were both working on the Seward Highway, Jim of Hodgkin's disease, Tucker of wounds in World War II.

I learned that he was born in Murray, Idaho, and his mother lived there until she died. He went back to visit often. His appearance signaled the arrival of the designated driver, and he would bring home uproarious stories of taking my Grandma Stoner and my great-aunt, Ruth

Aulbach, on road trips that began in Murray and ended in Spokane.

I wasn't smart enough to wonder why my grandmother's name was Stoner instead of Stabenow, and why my great-aunt's name was Aulbach. When I was twenty, he told me. Ruth's brother, Nathan, was my grandfather, but he had not married my grandmother. She had married somebody named Stabenow to give dad a name.

By that time I'd met Grandma Stoner, too. Grandma Stoner was short, hump-backed, eagle-beaked, fierce-eyed, tough, cantankerous, the least likely unwed mother I will ever meet. I was about to burst out laughing when I looked at Dad. He was pretending to root through a one-pound Darigold butter can for the right nut to thread on a bolt. He wasn't laughing. He was embarrassed, and ashamed. It was a thunderbolt to me, that he could be ashamed of such a thing, but for a man born in 1927 illegitimacy was no joke.

He never spoke of it again. I still don't know where the "Stoner" came from. It was only later that I recognized the pattern common to many who come to Alaska to build a new life. That life begins at the Beaver Creek border crossing. Anything that happens before is irrelevant. Anything that happens after is history. Dad was a master practitioner thereof.

This much I know: Too young to volunteer, Dad got Grandma Stoner to sign him into the merchant marine in time for the end of World War II. He was wounded off Okinawa in 1945, he thought by flak from one of our own anti-aircraft guns. "Shot in the ass by friendly fire," was how he invariably put it, and it made a better story anyway. He was still in the merchant marine when he came to Alaska the first time in 1945 on board a Liberty ship. He returned for good in 1947 on the Alaska-Canada Highway. In those days, the Royal Canadian Mounted Police stopped travelers at the Washington state-British Columbia border to check their supplies. "You were supposed to have two fan belts and a fuel filter and extra oil and water and gas and food and a bunch of other stuff," Dad said. The Mountie looked in the back seat of the Lincoln Zephyr, where Dad and his friend Omar "Mac" MacDonald had twenty gallons of gas, four cases of beer and two boxes of cheese crackers. "Shit, boys," the Mountie said, "if anybody makes it through, you will" and waved them on.

From the time he hit Alaska Dad was never out of work, except when he wanted to be. He started out as a laborer and worked his way up to master mechanic. He worked for Emil Usibelli and Cap Lathrop, helped build the Seward Highway, worked the Independence Mine the last winter it was open. He worked the Susitna gas fields, although he hated taking a helicopter to work; he was a fixed-wing man all the way. He drove a Cat train to Rampart in 1959, he worked on the trans-Alaska pipeline and half the subdivisions in Anchorage. When I was looking for a house in 1997, we'd turn a corner and he'd say, "Oh yeah, I helped lay the fill here. Check the wallboard, see if it's cracked."

One of the last things he said to me was, "I've always taken too much pride in a job well done to worry about my self-esteem."

Well, when he was on the job, sure. He held the world

record in getting fired, but that was because hunting and fishing and flying were more important to him than rebuilding the engine of a D-6 for Chugach Electric. In the fall, he'd call and say, "Hey, kid! I'm going hunting!" and I knew not to worry if I didn't hear from him for six weeks, instead of the three he had said he would be gone. "I was looking for work when I found this job," he said every time he got fired, and he was never out of work for any longer than he wanted to be.

He got his pilot's license at forty-two and from then on never owned less than one plane. "You can only fly one at a time, Dad," I pointed out when he acquired a Cessna 180 to go with the Piper Super Cub and the Cessna 172. "Yeah, but we can be in Naknek in an hour," he said. The phone would ring and it'd be "Hey, kid! I got a new plane! Wanna go for a ride?" I'd meet him at the Lake Hood float plane base or Merrill Field and we'd fly down to Polly Creek to go clamming or to Seldovia to visit friends or to Cordova to meet the shrimp boat or through Lake Clark Pass because it was there.

One sunny afternoon we took the Cub down the west side of Cook Inlet, sightseeing, looking at grizzlies fishing the Little Su, not flying too low over Tyonek. We landed to refuel and when we got back in the air the fumes from the funnel filled the cabin. I lasted as long as I could and then I smacked Dad and barked, "Put her down! NOW!" Dad hated anybody puking in his planes — during a previous flight he made a friend throw up into his own hip boot — and we plunked down on the bank of the Little Su and I bailed out before we'd stopped rolling.

Someone saw us make that abrupt descent and

landing, saw a woman jump out followed by a man, and took down the Cub's tail number. Three days later Dad called. "Hey, kid! You still alive? Good! The FBI wants to talk to you." This turned out to be the time of the Robert Hansen serial killings, and for a few sweaty hours one afternoon Dad was a possible suspect. "Took your time getting over here," Dad said when he answered the door. "Well, yeah," I said, and we both laughed.

Dad loved a joke, and he never loved a joke so much as when it was on him. The first time he wrecked a plane I asked him what happened. "It was a problem of vision," he said. "I had my head so far up my ass I couldn't see a thing."

He married four times. Although he would have denied it, he was a romantic. He liked to be in love, and he never lacked for female company. I understood the attraction he held for women. I also understood the divorces. Wives might change but his drinking and hunting and flying buddies never did, and they always came first.

It's easy to typecast these Alaskan old farts. Easy, but a mistake. Dad tithed to the Republican Party the way some people tithe to a church — I once saw a card inviting him to dinner at the Reagan White House — but one evening we were watching the news and a story came on about abortion protesters blockading a women's health clinic. The lead organizer was a man, and after the reporter interviewed him Dad said, "He can't get pregnant. It's none of his fucking business." You could have heard my jaw drop downtown.

He was always surprising me. I was raised with a half-

Aleut, half-Filipino family in Seldovia. The first time I met Dad he used the word "nigger." I was shocked, and I told him my friend Kathy was coming to visit me and that she had brown skin. He wasn't going to call her a nigger, was he? I was so in love with my brand-new father, and so hurt by this most grievous fault in him, and I was so afraid that my friend's feelings would be hurt, too. He heard me out in silence, and when Kathy came he never treated her with anything but respect and, afterward, genuine affection. Years later, long after I'd forgotten the incident, he told that story on himself, in company, to friends who were probably just as rednecked and bigoted as he was, watching me with a grin as he did so.

There was never a time when I could pigeonhole him, label him, file him safely away. He was always surprising me, always.

He wasn't religious, although he hoisted more than a few with Father Mike and he often told the story of watching Father Mike beat the shit out of a guy who had been beating on his wife the night before. He never attended church, and avoided all services except his own weddings. "What's the matter with them people?" he said once in what looked like genuine bewilderment, after he'd watched a news story on the Middle East. "They're neighbors, for Christ's sake, you'd think they had better things to do besides shooting at each other." His view was that the bullets would be better spent shooting caribou, or ptarmigan, or moose, although he stopped hunting moose when he started flying a Super Cub. It was a practical decision. You can't fit a whole moose into the back of a Super Cub. You can a whole caribou.

There was nothing Dad loved more than getting a bunch of friends together and cooking them food he'd killed himself, although he was never satisfied with the result. I remember one evening eight of us were eating ptarmigan he'd sautéed in butter and baked in wine. He took a bite and made a face. "Needs something else," he said. Whatever he cooked always needed something else, and I never figured out if he said it because he believed it or because he enjoyed the outcry that regularly followed. Maybe it was a little of both. One of the worst moments after he became ill was one evening when he said in real despair, "I can't even pick up a goddamn frying pan."

He liked verse, and after he died I leafed through his copy of Kipling's collected works. One of the dog-eared pages was "The Sons of Martha."

> It is their care in all the ages to take the buffet and cushion the shock.
> It is their care that the gear engages; it is their care that the switches lock.

A son of Martha, that was Dad. He could turn his hand to anything. He annualed his aircraft engines himself. He designed my raised-bed garden. He built a boat and used it to poach moose on Elmendorf Air Force Base. He turned a defunct gold mine into a fishing lodge. He recovered seven Nodwell tractors abandoned in the Bush by a United States Geological Survey team and rebuilt them and sold them. Every year for thirty-odd years he flew Outside, bought a car, drove it back over the Alcan, rebuilt it in Anchorage and sold it at enough of a profit to pay for his trip. His was the care that the gear engages. He made things work.

Lying bastard, he promised me he'd live to be 103. He died instead at 71, after a year's steadily increasing debilitation from some disease the doctors were never able to diagnose, and I can't even be angry at him that he reneged on our deal.

But that pedestal I put him on when I was fourteen? It's still there, and it's still pretty high.

Thorny Lieberman

Will Mayo is a tribal member of the Native village of Tanana. He lives in Fairbanks with Yvonne, his wife of twenty-five years, and has three children: Dustin, Christel and Angela.

The Hutlaanee Code

Will Mayo

My Indian name is *Saanh-Dlith-Toh'*. My English name is Will Mayo. I am a member of the Caribou Clan of the Koyukon Indian people and a citizen of the state of Alaska. I have two names because I walk in two worlds where the cultures are very different, as different as the names I bear.

My mother taught me in the Indian culture, all the while knowing that I would have to function in a world where that culture was unknown, and at times, in her experience, denigrated. As a girl she was punished for speaking her language in school. So the lesson was clear: Your Native tongue is bad and brings you pain. She never taught her children the language she speaks fluently. Other customs and traditions, such as Native dancing and singing or the potlatch ceremonies, were also judged to be unacceptable in modern American society and were banned.

In her Native village my mother contracted tuberculosis and was sent into the city for treatment, where she spent three years in the government hospital for Native people. She chose to settle in Fairbanks, where I was born in 1953. She told of how scared she was of white people. The big city was terrifying. I don't think she had felt so lonely since her mother died in the flu epidemic in the 1920s. It was not easy to be Indian and a single parent in the Fairbanks of the 1950s. Though she had her issues, she was determined that her children would face Alaskan culture outside the village without the aching dread that she herself had known.

In the Fairbanks public school system, I was educated with the same curriculum used across America, albeit with some uniquely Alaskan twists. I recall learning in the sixth grade that Alaskans are separated into two categories; one is either a "cheechako" (newcomer) or a "sourdough." Sourdoughs were immigrants who had been here a long time. There was no category for Natives. When I got home I proudly informed mom that I was a "sourdough," which earned me a funny little laugh. She told me that I was an Indian and we had always been in this land. I learned a small lesson but one that was a turning point in my self-understanding. I was an Alaska Native and my teacher did not know about us.

Something else occurred to me. Native people don't normally talk about how many years or how many generations they have lived in Alaska. Sourdoughs and pioneers talk about it quite a bit. To the Indian people such fine points of fact are unnecessary or superfluous. It is also possible that such recitations of one's tenure could be boastful, which would disrupt one's relationship to the land, the animals, and other people. It would therefore be considered *Hutlaanee* to do.

In spite of mom's wish to see her children educated in the new ways, being Indian was all she knew. The lessons her father had taught her were transmitted to me faithfully, if not always consciously. Much of my Indian education at home was delivered in a most succinct fashion. Warnings, actually, which were followed by a brief explanation of my transgression. These lessons were transmitted through the recitation of a single Indian word weighty with significance.

Upon the discovery that I was transgressing an ancient Indian law or social norm, I would hear that word uttered in various degrees of consternation, caution and reverence. The Indian word is *Hutlaanee* and it invokes the necessity for respectful behavior in all interactions with humans and with nature around us. It is heavy with admonition, warning and, at times, rebuke. It is also points one toward proper respect of what is sacred. It is steeped in an ancient code of conduct that is designed to keep the individual from making grave mistakes that would bring misfortune and calamity.

The keeping of the *Hutlaanee* code brings harmony. Breaking the ancient code was often disastrous, not only to the individual but, potentially, to the whole family or even community. There are some parts of the code that I cannot even reveal because to talk of them is a violation, except as a function of initial instruction. Even then the discussions are circumspect and delicately structured. Euphemisms and indirect references are used, for example, to instruct in behavior regarding certain animals or birds, or members of the opposite sex.

I suppose the word could best be described as a socio-religious term. It embodies the world view and theology of the Koyukon people of Interior Alaska, as well as the legal code of conduct in a small, close society.

The *Denaa nina'*, or the land of the people, is a most beautiful place, shrouded in a quiet that can bring tears to the eyes. It is also fraught with dangers and enveloped in a wondrous, though oft times harsh, climate. The *Denaa nina'* is beneficent but unforgiving of the foolish or un-prepared. Keeping the *Hutlaanee* code is more important than good hunting skills, well-made clothing, or well-balanced weapons. Survival is a full time job done well by the observant but impossible to achieve if the code is broken. Throughout my youth and adulthood I have been taught the *Hutlaanee* code and its lessons are with me daily in dozens of reminders both small and great.

As a modern Alaskan involved in routine interactions with the mainstream population, I have encountered numerous cultural intersections that are difficult to rec-oncile. Indeed, it is extremely difficult, though by no means impossible, for a Koyukon person to be true to the *Hutlaanee* code and achieve success in American business, political, or religious endeavors. For one who is reasonably adept in both the American way of doing things and in the *Hutlaanee* code the experience can be akin to whiplash of the soul, and requires certain accommodations our ancient elders would not find palatable or wise.

In the Koyukon culture of old, skillful speechmaking was the apex of intellectual achievement. It was a major component of any gathering of elders and chiefs. In old-time Koyukon speechmaking, the speaker would skillfully control inflection, volume, gestures and word usage to avoid violations of the *Hutlaanee* code. It was perfectly acceptable and admirable to harangue your audience using volume and gestures aggressively, as long as your content was in line with the code. Increasingly creative, extemporaneous word usage would stretch the limits of the abstract cognitive ability of the listeners until the speaker entered the realm of what the elders called the "high language" of the old people. A contest of wits and language skill would ensue in which successive speakers would "answer" the previous speaker with ever more powerful and poetic imagery, using increasingly abstract constructions. It was said of the best speechmaker that he had "sat down" his opponents, meaning no one could rise to challenge his eloquence, knowledge and skill. Only the most wise and skillful would even attempt to engage in these forums.

For this reason the art of speechmaking displayed much more than the ability to string words together. Such speakers were well versed in proper protocols and in the finer points of the *Hutlaanee* code. Foolish and careless use of words or the clumsy application of the code could bring many unpleasant consequences long after the gathering had concluded.

Public speaking is where I have encountered some of my greatest cultural conflicts. As a past elected leader among the tribes of Interior Alaska, I have made countless public addresses in different forums. The audiences have been varied and often mixed. The custom of introducing speakers with the recitation of a "bio" has been an area of conflict for me. It has the potential of violating the code if one prepares his own bio with the goal of impressing others. It can be a form of bragging about yourself.

When I first was asked to provide my bio for an

introduction I put everything in it, not thinking about how it would be used. When the emcee began reciting my background I became decidedly embarrassed and chagrined as the information was given voice. By the end of that introduction I had determined that I would not provide such a bio in the future. From that point on I wrote very short bios with a minimum of information to establish who I was for the benefit of audience.

It is said of one who is successful that they achieve success by being properly respectful, with appropriate humility regarding the task at hand. In modern English parlance the Indian uses the word "luck" to describe his success. It is important to note that the word "luck" as used in this context is designed to avoid bragging about one's success. A successful Koyukon hunter would never say, "I got this meat because I do not violate *Hutlaanee*." Such bragging would in itself be a violation, and you could lose your luck as a direct consequence. Usually nothing is said at all, but everyone knows why this success occurred. If forced to refer to it a hunter would simply say something like, "I had good luck today." Great care is taken not to attribute success to one's personal ability or skill, though others may do so on your behalf in certain circumstances.

The same concept holds true when *Hutlaanee* is superimposed on any human endeavor embarked upon by a Koyukon person in modern Alaskan society. A successful Koyukon businessperson who is observant of *Hutlaanee* would not predict or brag about success. Just as a Koyukon person would not say, "I am going out to get my moose so you better get the frying pan ready" neither would he say he is going to "make this business deal happen so you better break out the party hats."

I share this as just one facet of the *Hutlaanee* code. Of course, this code is not followed by every Koyukon person one hundred percent. Modern American culture is replacing much of the traditional practice in this regard. I have caught myself using methods and saying things that violate the code, but I try hard not to make it a practice.

There are a couple of incidents I can share where my violation of the code or my adherence to the code was rewarded with appropriate consequences.

In traditional Koyukon culture it was not permitted for a man to utilize any article of women's clothing for any purpose related to their role in the community or family. As a twelve-year-old I owned a rifle and I was very proud of this weapon. I took real good care of it, making sure it was clean inside and out after every use. On one occasion I had run out of cleaning patches and went looking all over the house for a suitable replacement. I found an article of clothing that my mom no longer needed as much as I did. I used it to clean my .22, thinking of how clever I was to find this replacement. I had removed all the inner mechanisms for a thorough cleaning but when I tried to reassemble the weapon I broke one of the delicate, key components. I was devastated because we were very poor and I had no idea how to fix it and no money to get it repaired. At that point, my mom came into the house to see the article of women's clothing beside my cleaning kit and she spoke the word, "*Hutlaanee.*" She explained that for a man to touch his weapon with a woman's clothes would ruin his luck and the weapon would no longer be useful in providing food and protection. At that point she did not know that I had broken my .22 and I did not want to tell her. That was one experience.

The next one I will share is when I was hunting moose. One evening during the hunting season I decided to go for a ride with my rifle to "look around." A Koyukon hunter is never supposed to announce that he is going out to get moose. Instead he says, "I am going to look around," and the fact that he has his rifle lets everybody know what is happening. The reason is that, in the traditional way, if you indicate that you are going to be successful in your hunting of moose before you go out, you will ruin your luck. It is *Hutlaanee.*

I got in my truck and drove out of town a few miles to a popular road hunting area. There were hunters everywhere, driving up and down the road looking into the woods. Road hunting gets ridiculous close to town but I didn't have any option since I had to leave town for business and this was going to be my only chance to hunt that fall.

Anyway, there were trucks in front of me and in back most of the evening. I decided to just go home since there were too many people looking around. As I headed back home I found myself alone on a stretch of road when a moose suddenly ran across the road in front of me. I stopped beside the road about a hundred yards away and walked into the woods. I looked down to see the moose slowly walking among the birch trees but mostly hidden. I took a shot and immediately began running full speed toward where I saw him. He was nowhere in sight. I decided to continue running down into the woods thinking I might get another chance at a shot if I spotted him. I ran and ran deeper into the forest but no moose was in sight. I heard brush crashing behind me, stopped, and turned. There, right in my footsteps and only fifteen yards behind me, the moose was following me into the forest. He stopped and slowly turned sideways and I had a perfect shot. I took the shot and the moose went down.

Later, when I got my mom to come and help me get the good parts from the moose guts, she told me that this moose was honoring me and wanted me to get him. That was why he crossed the road when no one else was around and why he then followed on my heels as I ran through the woods away from him.

For whatever reason, I had good luck that day. I believe God blessed me just like he blessed the children of Israel when they were in the desert after they left Egypt. God brought thousands of birds across their path for them to eat and they were easy to get. He brought a nice young bull to the road for me that day. I needed the meat so badly and I had no other chance to go hunting that year. In the Koyukon language God is *Denaahuto'*. In our traditional way the elders would say that I was blessed as an indication that I kept my luck through respectful observance of the *Hutlaanee* code. (I hope by saying this that I am not bragging and therefore have to face consequences.)

In Alaska there are many different beliefs. They continue side-by-side in daily life but many people do not have a clue that they are there. Some have been in place for untold generations, others for just a couple of hundred years. I think God has revealed Himself in many different ways to the peoples of the earth whom He loves. He would like it if we loved one another.

Courtesy of the author

Larry Campbell is a general assignment metro reporter with the Anchorage Daily News *and has taught journalism at the University of Alaska Anchorage.*

The Color of Opportunity

Larry Campbell

We were all at the dinner table that evening — me, my mom and dad, and my brother. I was twelve. Russ was nine. We could hardly sit still. Dad had just gotten back from Washington, D.C. We wanted to hear all about it — the town, the monuments, the promotion he'd been offered. We wanted to hear him say, "Well, we're moving to D.C." Oh, man, I couldn't wait.

"Well, boys, your mother and I have been talking, and …." Dad's elbows rested on the table and his fingers were woven together. He wasn't smiling. "Well, we don't think were going to move."

I felt a lump in my throat. I looked at Russ and there were tears welling in his eyes. The nation's capital. It had been all we could think about since Dad had flown back there a week before.

"How come?" I asked in a quiet voice.

"Well, because of the places we'd have to live. The neighborhoods. Well, boys, it's just not the places we think would be good for you guys."

He didn't say any more. He didn't have to. We knew the kinds of neighborhoods Dad was talking about. We knew them from visit to relatives in the Lower 48. Dirty, dark expanses of cracked pavement with broken windows in every house, and bare, brown lawns and mangy dogs with mean barks behind bare wood picket fences. Neighborhood kids in filthy clothes with filthy mouths. Scary-looking men who walked around in the middle of the day because they didn't have jobs. The slums.

Our neighborhood in Anchorage was the opposite. Clean streets, clipped lawns, well-kept houses with trees and back yards. Kids who laughed and had bicycles. Dads who pulled station wagons into driveways at day's end.

In Anchorage in 1967, we could choose what neighborhood we wanted to live in. In any other big city, the neighborhood would choose us. Dad was black. Mom is mulatto; that's half black, half white. That makes me and my siblings three-quarters black. But at the dinner table that night, after Dad got back from the nation's capital, I felt all black.

And that's why we lived in Alaska.

Mom and Dad met and married in Portland, Oregon, and moved to Seattle. Dad had been a pilot in the Army Air Corps, a Tuskegee airman, and he was the first black man ever to fly a military fighter jet. Flying became his livelihood.

In Seattle he joined the Civil Aeronautics Board, which later became the National Transportation Safety Board. His job was investigating airplane accidents. Only problem was he never got sent out on any. All the other investigators got to go out to the crash scenes. Dad sat in the office filling out paperwork. He knew why.

When a spot for an investigator opened in Alaska, Dad applied. Alaska, where there were almost as many pilots' licenses as there were drivers' licenses. Surely they must have crashes up there.

He got the job, a two-year stint in the Anchorage office. I remember walking down the stairs from the Northwest Orient Airlines Boeing 707 in January 1963. Russ and I just started running across the ramp toward the single-story terminal at Anchorage International. Our little lungs froze before we ran fifty feet. Dad picked us up, one under each arm: "Cold, isn't it?" Russ and I grinned.

Seems like Dad had to leave almost before we got unpacked. Before a year was done, he'd been to more places in the state than most residents, exotic locales like Galena, Fort Yukon, Kotzebue, Kodiak, Bethel, Nome. Everywhere a pilot flew, Dad eventually went. He was one of only three accident investigators for the entire state. Dad went out into the field all the time. He loved it. He applied to stay another two years.

Russ and I were starting to like it, too. We walked a mile down Fireweed Lane to North Star Elementary School. Sometimes we walked along the ridges of the snow berms like mountaineers. Going to school was an adventure. Just living here was an adventure. It was like the moon, but with movie theaters.

Dad had joined the Air National Guard in Washington state and stayed with it in Alaska. Kulis Air National Guard Base became a second job. He was chief pilot when the Good Friday earthquake hit in 1964. He was Gov. Bill Egan's pilot when the governor visited the tsunami-ravaged towns of Valdez, Seward, Cordova and Kodiak. It was an important position, and Dad was the best pilot they had.

Mom tried to like Alaska, but she wasn't quite as happy. Her soap operas aired two weeks late. Back then, tape-delay broadcasts really meant something. There was no Bon Marché or Lippmans department store. The most popular department store here was named after an animal — Caribou's. She missed her parents and brothers and sisters. All had been within an easy, three-hour drive from Seattle to Portland. She clung to her familiar Safeway grocery and wished for a Fred Meyer.

That was one of the reasons Dad seriously considered moving to D.C. It was the late 1960s, the height of the civil rights movement. Dad was one of just a handful of blacks in the Civil Aeronautics Board. They wanted to show him off where he'd be seen. He knew what they were thinking, but it was a promotion. And Mom liked the idea of moving back to "the states."

I could tell Dad was pretty disappointed at the dinner table that night. None of us talked for the rest of dinner. No one finished his plate. Dad hardly talked the rest of the evening and just went to the living room after dinner and watched television.

Instead of living in the midst of the era, we let television bring us the assassinations of Robert Kennedy and Martin Luther King, the 1968 Democratic National Convention in Chicago, the race riots in Watts. The movie "Shaft" and the music of Isaac Hayes was as close as we got to the kind of neighborhood that Dad came from, and that his brothers still lived in back in Portland. In Alaska's cold seclusion we watched the evolution of the movement. We never said it out loud, but I think all of us — Mom, Dad, me and Russ — were glad we were here and not there.

I had a friend at Dimond High School, an acquaintance actually. He was more black than me and his skin was darker. Like me, he grew up mostly in Anchorage. His father went into local politics, first the school board, then the state legislature. (It'd probably be unfair to link his success to local reactions to the civil rights battles we all saw on the TV news. But who knows what goes on in the heads of some white folk?)

Anyway, my friend started taking on some of the mannerisms we saw on TV and in the movies. He started walking the walk and talking the talk. He grew an Afro. He raised his fist and shouted, "Black Power," at high school pep rallies while everybody else was shouting, "Go, Dimond." He tried to get me to do the same. I wouldn't. One day he came up to me in the hall and said: "You know, Larry. You better get with it. You can't 'pass' all your life. It's gonna be coming up here, y'know? The Movement. Power to the People. You can't be white, Larry. You aren't white. You gotta choose, Larry. You gotta choose someday."

That pissed me off. I didn't want to choose. Nothing that I knew in my life made me think I had to. What's the matter with this guy? H. Rap Brown? Malcolm X? Man, they're all just images on TV. They're "down there." We're up here, in Alaska. Our dads have nice jobs. We live in nice neighborhoods. We've got cars and money to buy gas. We're getting good grades in school. Jeez, man, what is your problem with all this? He and I never talked after that.

But you know that old saying: "You can run, but you can't hide"? Ignorant rednecks found their way to Alaska like cockroaches in the late 1960s and early 1970s, on the barges and cargo carriers bringing new waves of people chasing the newly discovered oil wealth.

Then there was that thing with a girlfriend's father: "But honey, he's black!" Dad had a run-in with a supervisor who the National Transportation Safety Board transferred up from the South. He eventually won an anti-discrimination complaint, but he left the board shortly afterward. The fight had exhausted his enthusiasm.

But, y'know, those things never broke my family's affinity for this place. Dad became commander of the Air Guard base for awhile, the first black to command an Air Guard base in the country. Mom's knitting was beginning to win ribbons at the state fair and Fur Rendezvous competitions. My folks even produced three more kids in this state. I found new girlfriends. Russ and I played in rock bands, covering Led Zeppelin and Grand Funk Railroad. God, life was great.

Nearly forty years later, Mom and Dad's decision to keep the family in Alaska seems even more prophetic to me. They must've known that, despite the cold and the isolation and the two-week-old TV soaps, something would be more different in this country than anywhere else in the nation. I see my parents' blind wisdom more clearly each year, especially now that I'm a father myself.

I think they chose well. I know they did. Because I don't think I'd be so willing to tell you my life's story if I'd grown up in D.C. 🪶

Courtesy of the author

Susan Alexander Derrera, a finalist for the Modern Poetry Association's 2000 Ruth Lilly Fellowship, is a high school English teacher, writer, and mother of Alexandra and Aidan.

Augusts in Juneau

Susan Alexander Derrera

I am lying under a heavy rose-dappled quilt in a narrow twin bed on the landing outside my grandparents' bedroom door in a small wood-framed house on Twelfth Street in Juneau. A light in the stairwell sends shadows across the room. I breathe in the smell of Vicks and cool night rain. Car tires whisk through the wet streets outside my window as my grandfather's old Baby Ben with the winder like a metal wing tick tick ticks the time away in the room next door.

My father is somewhere with me, but I'm not sure exactly where. I just hear his voice. He is telling me the story of Rumpelstiltskin and tonight I have managed to stay awake for his performance of the dwarf's angry tirade once the miller's daughter correctly "guesses" his name. I love his stories, how he can recall them without the aid of books — something no one else I know can do — how the words color the darkness and my loneliness, and how the solid deck of his voice can ferry me gently to sleep. I do not know at this moment that I am becoming a writer, but I am — listening, observing, storing images and sounds. Surprisingly, given the love I have for my father's storytelling, I will not become a creator of fiction, of other worlds. My interests have always been in the one world I was given; long before I took up a pen and wrote a poem, I have been trying to plumb it.

"Good night, honey," he says when the story is done. He kisses me, then leaves. I hear the stairs creak and groan under his weight. I listen for the heavy click of the old light switch that darkens the stairwell. Then I scramble from my bed, perch myself at the dormer window, and watch my father's back as he walks down the short path that takes him away from the house. I notice the skin of his neck, bare and bulging over his tweed sportcoat. The soles of his shoes scratch against the wet cement as he disappears into the darkness.

My parents divorced when I was just beginning to put language to use. I have no memory of them together and only came to know them separately, in their own distinct landscapes. Every August from the time I was three years old, I was sent to see my father in Juneau, six hundred air miles away from my mother and the rest of my family at our house by the lake in the small town of Wasilla in southcentral Alaska. I had no choice. I stayed at my grandmother's house, first on the landing, and later in my mother's childhood bedroom. There, disconnected from the comforts of my familiar life, I learned the meaning of longing, before I knew it was a place out of which art can come.

A day seemed longer in Juneau. Those years of

Augusts were so much the same and the rain, its sad rhythm, echoed my soul's weather. I filled the hours in the company of my grandparents, my father, and mostly by myself, learning how to be with the writer's most essential company.

"Sue-sun," Grandma calls, my name sounding uncomfortable on her Norwegian tongue. "Sue-sun. Get up."

I am ten or eleven now, waking in my mother's bedroom, a place where I have imagined her at my age every time I've slept there. It is a small room papered over with lavender flowers and green vines. The wood floors are polished to a high gloss. A doily lies on top of an equally glossy dresser-top. The room smells pleasantly old, like the inside of a hatbox. It is late morning.

"Coming, Grandma," I yell from a sitting position, hoping that will help my voice carry.

Downstairs in the kitchen, my grandfather wipes an oiled cloth around the surface of a cast-iron skillet. He pours thin creamy batter into the pan, tips it this way and that, and returns it to the stove. He brings me the hot pancake draped over a narrow spatula and flips it onto my plate. I spread the margarine, the Mapeline, roll up the pancake, and eat silently, my fingers sticky on the handle of the fork. My grandmother sits across from me dressed in one of her slippery nylon dresses with the zipper up the front that she always wears to work in the housekeeping department at St. Ann's, the hospital where I was born on the day Alaskans voted to accept the statehood bill. Her formidable aqua bosom nearly rests on the table. Several pancakes later, she speaks.

"Have you had your b.m.?" She is obsessed with bodily functions, symptoms, disease.

"Not yet, Grandma," I finally respond in an embarrassed whisper.

Silence again as she watches me eat. Grandpa flips another pancake onto my plate. His sleeve smells of wet wool and drying halibut line. The radio on the kitchen windowsill is broadcasting "Problem Corner," but the signal isn't completely clear. A woman is trying to sell a baby crib. Another is looking for a job; she can mend fish nets.

"You make sure you get your education," my grandmother suddenly pronounces. "A man will always leave you."

I look at my grandfather, Emil, dipping his sugar cube into the fragrant coffee that covers a landscape in the bottom of a Blue Willow cup. I know she is not referring to him, although in ten years, he too will die and leave her, but to my mother's father, Olaf, who built this house in 1916 on a flat piece of land between the saltwater channels of the Inside Passage and the narrow, hilly streets leading up to Mount Juneau and Mount Roberts. He built the bedroom I just left where my mother lay when she was just a few years older than I am, listening through the walls to her father's slow death from colon cancer. It pains me to think of her there, tossing in grief-soaked dreams.

"Okay, Grandma," I say, relieved to have the last pancake finished. I kiss my grandfather on the cheek, his face as rough as his wool shirt, and thank him for breakfast. He fumbles in his Filson trouser pocket and slips me a dollar when he's sure my grandmother isn't looking. I kiss him again and yell to my grandmother that I'll be back before dinner.

I am ready for my daily walk downtown ("uptown," my mother called it in the diary she kept when she was nine: "went uptown to get a flower for John Krugness. He is sick.") I am going to see my father at his shop, a photography studio and darkroom on Front Street he has occupied since the mid-1950s. Drafted from his Chicago home in the summer of 1941 for what was supposed to be only a six-month tour of duty, he was sent to Juneau to establish a camp, document its construction, and operate a darkroom following the Japanese invasion of the Aleutians. He met my mother at one of the lodge hall dances held regularly for the servicemen. I can see why he was attracted to her. Once, when I was browsing through one of his old Kodak paper boxes, I found a glossy close-up of Ingrid Bergman he took when she and Dashiell Hammett came to entertain the troops. Her luminous skin and pale clear eyes looked just like my mother's

The brass doorknob for the front door is a little loose; it rattles in the fixture before it engages. The porch smells of open umbrellas and wet newsprint; rain runs down the rippled window glass. I open the porch door, put the hood up on my raincoat, and walk down the pocked cement steps edged with moss, toward the gate that divides the Siberian pea hedge from the sidewalk.

Click, click, rattle goes the C-shaped hand of the gate, cold and slippery with rain. I lock the gate again and wipe my wet hand on my pant leg. The sharp green smell of the newly trimmed hedge follows me up Twelfth Street. I walk these streets every day, not with the easy confidence of one who lives here nor with the casual interest of the tourist, but more like one briefly exiled who carefully regards the place that has taken her in, all the while hoping for glimpses of the familiar, the beloved. Home.

Head down, I count the star-studded water meter boxes manufactured in Indiana. Even then they looked old, from a time long before I first walked here. I have to watch my step: there are dips and cracks in the sidewalk. In places, the top layer of concrete is completely worn, revealing beautiful milky rocks locked in a river of cement.

At the top of Twelfth, I cross the street and hop over a curb worn like the edge of an old shoe. When I reach the bridge over Gold Creek, I stop and lean on the cement overlook to watch the creek water run. Soon it will reach the channel, kiss the hull of my grandfather's boat, surround Douglas Island that lies off shore, and reach the open ocean.

Dizzy from watching the water moving so rapidly down the cleavage of the canal, I leave the overlook and the prickly scent of hollow-stemmed devil's club to head up the hill on Calhoun. It is cool and dark under the large branches of spruce and mountain ash. I am a little winded and my thighs are starting to burn when I quickly glance for traffic and cross the street. From here I can see the Stewarts' large brown house. It always looks vacant as most of the houses in Juneau eerily do. One of the girls is my age. I played with her once in her bedroom, Tom Jones' "Pussycat, Pussycat, woe-oh-woe-oh-woe-oh," spinning on the record player in the corner. My grandmother thought she was a bad influence, but then she thought most children were. Rarely did I meet or play with a child my own age.

When I was younger, I tagged along with my grandparents learning the careful art of observation. I stood quietly by at the cold storage while my grandfather visited with his woolly fisherman friends, and with my grandmother at her widowed friend's apartment that always smelled of liniment and the soiled newspapers that line the bottoms of bird cages.

I remember going with my grandmother to get her hair done every week. Her hairdresser, Abbie Jane, kept a Christmas tree up year-round — you could see it from the street, a dusty silver garland circling it and reflecting the colored ornaments and blinking lights. Sitting across from my grandmother in the back of the hairdresser's house, the air thick with the strong fumes of permanent wave solution, I watched my grandmother through stinging eyes. Neck resting on the edge of the pink hairdresser's sink, I could see the gold in her back teeth and her thin, sparse hair slicked wet against her scalp. I flipped through a magazine, the pages turning different colors as the tree lights blinked on and off, hoping I would never grow old.

I remember holding my grandfather's hand, thick as a bear's paw, while he walked me down to the boat harbor to check on his boat, the *Dixon*, an immaculate wooden trawler. He was so scrupulously clean that it's hard to believe he ever picked up a habit like chewing snuff, but he did. He spit the juice into a Folgers coffee can that he carried around with him everywhere, indoors and out. The

Copenhagen smelled wonderful, like fine wet leather. The scent clung to him, like the faint smell of diesel, weathered wood, and dry halibut line that was caught in the weave of his clothes.

I walk on, my right elbow almost touching the walls of the houses as I pass them. I wonder what goes on inside these homes with narrow sidewalks for yards, try to imagine lives that aren't mine.

Near the governor's mansion, I make a quarter turn to allow room for a stranger to pass going in the opposite direction. Years before I was born, my mother was Gov. Ernest Gruening's chief assistant; she used to go to parties at the mansion. I can picture her there in a smart new dress she made just the night before from a Vogue pattern. I picture my father inside, out of place until he begins to arrange the players for photographs, temporarily controlling the scene.

The fire horn blows its mournful two-pitched wail. I stop to listen. It's only signaling the hour. Noon.

A little farther down Calhoun, a small wooden overpass stretches across the pavement. Hanging in the living room in Wasilla is an early painting by Juneau artist Rie Muñoz that my mother bought at an art show in the Elks Hall when she was pregnant with me. In the painting, several kerchiefed girls and wool-capped boys mount the steps to the simple bridge; others are already crossing it as I am about to do now on my way to the library at Fourth and Main. My mother's father, Olaf, helped construct the overpass in the early 1930s, when he was street commissioner for the city; he was worried about the safety of the children who had to cross the busy street on their way to school. Even though I have never met this grandfather, I feel I know him by his works. I believe I would have loved him very much.

The glass pane in the basement door of the library rattles when the door closes. The sound of the rain outside is muffled. The library smells of glue and typewriter ribbons. I peruse the shelves, pulling out books somewhat aimlessly. From the back of the books, I take out the thick yellowing cards from their sleeves and look for my mother's name. Finally I check out *Cherry Ames: Student Nurse* to read later at the shop or back at my grandmother's where my mother recorded in her diary the books she read in January of 1931: *Barbara Winthrop at Boarding School*; *Barbara Winthrop at Camp*; *When Patty Went to College*.

I walk past the marble-pillared Capitol Building where my mother worked for so many years for Governor Gruening before I was born, then cross Seward Street, turn right and go down, down, down, my toes hitting against the inside of my wet tennis shoes. I go past Behrends Department Store where Grandma buys the red socks she sends me every Christmas ("Red goes with everything") and where my mother sat in the window on election day in 1958 with me on her lap, a get-out-the-vote effort to elect Alaska's first legislature and congressional representatives.

Some days I stop to help Inez Gregg, the small gray-haired proprietor of the Baranof Book Store. She lets me stock shelves. I love touching the books. The glue on the spine makes a small cracking sound when a book is opened; some pages are cool and glossy, others thick as construction paper, the ink bleeding into the loose fibers. When no one is looking, I bury my nose in them, breathe the intoxicating scent of their woody, inky bodies. Today I just look in the door and wave at Inez. She is behind the counter ringing up a purchase on the register. A ribbon of white tape runs down the front of the counter, gently curling at the bottom.

Back on the street, I cross Second and stop to look in the window of Ann's, a children's clothing store where some of my baby clothes were purchased — the special ones, like the pink wool coat and bonnet I was wearing in a photograph taken shortly after my first birthday. Farther down the block, in the display window at Hudson's Shoes, I admire a pair of navy blue suede loafers with one-inch stacked heels. Reluctantly, I leave them behind to go into the drugstore on the corner. I pick up a *Betty & Veronica* comic book and a pack of Black Jack gum. Before purchasing them, I go to the cosmetics area and find a thick white pot of the Pacquin hand cream that my mother always uses after she washes the dishes. I open it, breathe in the scent of her soft dewy hands.

Out on Front Street, a group of noisy ravens has convened, talking in strident, haunting voices. I tread carefully around their space and, finally, reach the shop. It is another world inside, the place where my father spends most of his life, where time is always getting briefly stopped — captured on paper — through his art.

A trio of brass bells makes a clunky ring when I open the door. Moments later, my father appears from the back of the shop, greeting me as if it's been twelve months, rather than twelve hours, since he last saw me. "Honey," he croons. Behind him, on the highest display shelf are two hand-tinted photographs of me in a pale blue sailor dress taken the first summer I was sent to see him.

I put my library book and comic book on a chair, shake out of my raincoat, and give my dad a quick summary of my day so far. He listens with interest and returns to the back.

Three distinct areas divide the shop. The front section is designed for the customer and the transaction of business. It smells of Windex and Aqua Net hairspray. Against the walls are various multi-layered shelving units displaying his work. There's Miss Juneau touching a leaf at the Evergreen Bowl, there's a grouping of senior portraits, class of 1969 stickers situated in the bottom corners, there's a group shot of a Little League team, the Mendenhall Glacier rising behind it. When I was younger, I stood on a rubber-topped stepstool, punching numbers on the cash register, writing out make-believe receipts, and fetching my father when a customer appeared, usually a woman collapsing her umbrella in the red glow of the neon "Alexander Photo" sign reflecting backwards off the tile floor.

The middle area of the shop is set up for sittings. The floor is a dangerous, snaky pool of electrical cords and rolling, three-clawed lights. A narrow bookcase holds lenses, film packs, and props for children — a squeaky rubber Kewpie doll, a small red ball, a gray kitten puppet. My father's gentle way, his fairy tale voice, draws children to him; they smile readily in his presence.

Toward the back of this space, a heavy maroon drape

hangs opposite a large mirror where customers always comb their hair, touch up, prepare for the pose by which they want to be remembered, before my father and his camera do their time-altering, image-altering work.

At a desk in the back, a densely packed area that comprises the final part of the shop, my father sits staring through an enormous magnifying glass at a negative he is retouching. His eyes water in the bright light shining up from the base of the retoucher. Sharp Ticonderoga pencils are lined up on the desk. He picks one up and with the lightest stroke of carbon, erases a wrinkle.

To keep me occupied, he hands me a large gold Kodak paper box, hairy black fringe on the bottom where the seal was broken. It is filled with flawed prints that are fun to study: figures caught a moment before or after expecting to be caught; informal party scenes; domestic interiors. All these reveal more than the carefully crafted portraits. In one of the prints, my father has inked Vandyke beards and horns on a few of the men and a circle of rays around my mother's eyes; next to her image he's written "Bedroom Eyes," which I don't quite understand. I commence with my "work," taking the prints, one by one, and putting them through the paper cutter, slicing one edge, rotating it a quarter turn, slicing, rotating, slicing, rotating, until the print is the size of a gray postage stamp, a strange sort of editing I enjoy.

That done, he hands me another box of ocher-colored three-by-three negatives. I open the door next to the desk and enter the darkroom to make prints. I sit on a metal stool at the contact printer in the dim amber light, open the box of negatives, place one on the printer, lay a fresh sheet of light-sensitive paper on top of it, and press the metal top down. Intermittently, a drop of water plunks into a full tray of pure H_2O in the developing sink. I lift the metal top and remove the paper where an image has been recorded, still invisible to me. In the silence and the darkness, I learn one way through which images can arrive, through which transience can be captured.

Promptly at five o' clock, my father closes the shop. Together, we walk to the Elks Club, just around the corner on Franklin Street. On the way, his eyes pan the ground looking for coins, for treasure. He nearly always finds something — metal zipper pulls, fishing swivels, gold rings, lost knobs from car dashboards. He keeps the coins, but when he's acquired a significant cache of the other, he bundles them up in an envelope and, when I am back home in Wasilla, sends them to me in the mail, labeled "Found Jewelry." Inside the package, the formerly lost, random, trampled objects take on a new luster. I lay them out on my bedspread and study them, amazed at how I would never have noticed them had they not been adrift, without place or meaning until my father picked them up and gave them to me as gifts. I think about what this means, about all the people symbolically represented on my bedspread by what they have unknowingly or regretfully lost.

In the reading room at the Elks Club, my father reads the newspaper in a slippery looking overstuffed green chair and sips a draught beer, the foam sticking to his upper lip. I pull old Totem yearbooks from the book-shelves and search through the pages for glimpses of my mother, my aunts. I sip a Shirley Temple through a red translucent bar straw and turn the cool, shiny pages slowly, looking for her name. The delicate sound of one billiard ball striking another slips through the air. Finally, I find her. In her senior portrait, she looks like something out of a Maxfield Parrish painting: tight wave in her hair, full lips, luminous eyes. "Katherine Torkelsen was very active in high school dramatics, musical affairs, and class affairs," it reads.

After their divorce my father moved to an efficiency apartment on the fifth floor of the Mendenhall Apartments, an eight-story building on the corner of Fourth and Franklin, just a few blocks up the street from the Elks Club. I must have stayed with him there once, as I remember sleeping on a narrow cot at night and in the morning looking out at Gastineau Channel from his formica-covered kitchen table, a bowl of Kellogg's Frosted Flakes growing soggy in front of me. But most of the time, I just visited him there briefly, long enough for him to freshen up for dinner at my grandmother's or to fetch something he'd forgotten before going to the bowling alley.

While there, I liked to rummage through his desk and reread the cards I'd written him, my handwriting more refined each year. For a special treat, he'd set up his reel to reel tape recorder, thread the shiny brown tape onto the reels, and push "play," my four-year-old voice captured long ago, now miraculously filling the tiny apartment.

The efficiency was so small there was no room for a bed. A gray tweedy sofa-sleeper parked against one wall was the only piece of living room furniture in the place.

He pulled it out at night and pushed it back in the morning for more than thirty years.

We leave the Elks and walk up the three blocks to the Mendenhall's outdoor parking lot, where my father keeps his car, a green Impala, that we drive over to Grandma's for dinner. When we get there, she is at the kitchen stove, a fork in hand, ready to turn a small piece of halibut in a shallow layer of sizzling oil at the bottom of the cast-iron frypan. Grandpa is in his chair, reading the *Juneau Empire* that's delivered at five o'clock on weekdays. His Folgers can is on the floor next to the chair.

I wash up in the bathroom with a bar of Ivory soap grown thin. Gray cracks that aren't dirt split it apart as the soap rotates in my hands.

"Dinner," Grandma calls. "It's hot. Come right now."

At the round oak table we eat off of sunny, yellow Fiestaware plates that were a wedding gift to my parents.

"Yoe," my grandmother says, the English "j" still impossible for her to pronounce after more than fifty years. "Here," and she passes him the serving dishes: steaming boiled potatoes, orange Jell-O filled with grated carrots, canned corn heated in a saucepan, halibut caught and filleted by my grandfather now beautifully golden, fried in the lightest egg batter. A plastic lemon for squeezing on the fish is in the center of the table.

On a little wooden stand behind the dinner table, on the front of the Juneau-Douglas phonebook, my grandmother has written my father's two phone numbers in her rounded European script. Even when I am not here, she looks after him. It gladdens me.

After dinner we might have vanilla ice cream brought up from the Cold Spot in the basement, or a bowl of fresh peaches in thick cream, or my favorite, a concoction of leftover rice, sugar, and cream which I called "Snow on the Mountain." Then, we might play Old Maid or checkers, visit my godparents, or — as we will this night — go down to the ten-lane Channel Bowl to bowl a few games.

The alley smells of cooking grease and fresh floor wax and the sweaty fingerholes in a bowling ball. I pick out an eight-pounder, put on the worn out bowling shoes with fraying laces, and wait at the lane for my father to come back from his locker in the basement. The rackety, explosive sound of pins scrambling echoes off the advertisements lining the walls of the alley.

He brings me a cream soda from the vending machine and writes our names on the thin scoresheet with the chubby eraserless Brunswick pencil. "Susie." "Daddy Joe." I marvel at how quickly he can add numbers from frame to frame, even after three strikes. To remove a rare error he wets his index finger, nail stained yellow from developing chemicals, and rubs it against the flimsy fibrous paper marked up with dark graphite.

After a few games, we drive back to Grandma's; he walks me to the door, pushes my hair behind my ears, and kisses me goodnight. I wonder when he last kissed someone other than me, wonder how long a person can live without being touched.

My grandparents have already gone to bed, so I climb the stairs on tiptoe and quietly close the door to my mother's bedroom. A large Pan Am calendar brushes against the door. August is almost over. Between the cool sheets and the nubby chenille bedspread, I read from the stack of comic books I relocate every year in the attic: *Little Dot*, *Little Lotta*, *Little Audrey*, and my favorite, *Millie the Model*, whose foot has my mother's high arch.

When I turn out the small, shaded light over the headboard, I think of my grandparents sleeping in the next room in their bed that smells of flannel and wool and some musky dampness caught in the folds of their skin. I think of my father across town in his hide-a-bed, the apartment dark, the clock radio on for company. It is two hours earlier in Wasilla and I wonder what my family is doing. Are they missing me, too? In answer, I hear the clatter of dishes and conversation, see the northern light still spilling across the dinner table, find the routine maintained in spite of the empty chair. I feel almost dead in one place, dreadfully conscious in the other. Ardently, I wish for some sort of transporting power to take me away or at least to make me feel at home in this place, my mother's land, but not my own. I don't yet know that what I am really wishing for is a voice.

It would be years before I found poetry, but when I did, I knew I had been strongly preparing for it all my life, and formatively in those quiet lonely Augusts spent searching for connections to who I was and where I belonged. Still, of course, there is longing and a new longing now: to do it right as I take up the work of a grandfather I never knew — becoming, like him, a builder of houses, small bridges. Poems. Something in which to live a life. Something to save one. 🪵

Mark Daughhetee

Juneau-born Dan DeRoux is married with two step-children, and has a studio with a wonderful view of the Chilkat Mountains.

Leaving in Alaska

Dan DeRoux

If you ask me, living in Alaska is like being a sliver in someone's finger. You will eventually work your way out. Even if you didn't plan on it, you'll find yourself exiting. It's a subtle mental health mechanism to protect us from going completely nuts. You could get soaked out, or if you are really annoying, you might even get tweezed. I love living here but I would be on vacation for half of the year if I could. We have wonderful friends and everyone agrees we'd all like to be gone for half of the year, but no one wants to be without his friends. We haven't figured that out yet.

I was born in Alaska in 1951. I began painting twenty years later. Thirty years later I am still painting. That's what I do. I've been cursed. I live in the most stupendously magnificent landscape in the world, and I'm not a landscape painter. Not the usual kind anyway. I look at the landscape and it's very pretty, but I'll imagine that it's been inhabited by the Dutch, or the Italians, and it suddenly becomes much more interesting to me. Mount

Juneau will still be there, but I'll see canals where the streets are, and the third-rate architecture is replaced by villas or palaces. I would love to be on the city planning commission.

The same thing happens to me with art history, though I have an Alaskan's view of it: The Madonna as a walrus, her children digging clams for her. The Venetians will be landing a whale, Sargent's Flamenco dance will be to the beat of Eskimo drummers, Rembrandt's Syndics will be in Tlingit regalia. Then again, I can forget Alaska altogether and have a dream adventure with Maxfield Parrish and Dagwood Bumstead. I don't like to boast, but I am a great escape artist. I can transport myself not only across continents, but through time.

I don't like to hunt. Fishing is all right. I don't ski but I'll get in a couple of hikes every summer. I think I'm a typical Alaskan. Most of the folks I know who are avid outdoorsmen are transplants. Tourists have seen way more than I have and if I were one I'd probably do the same. Imagine… "Wow, what a cool mountain, let's run up and look around!" Or, "Hey, look at all that pristine snow, let's ski across it!"

One reason the outdoor life is so minimal here in Juneau is because it seems to be constantly raining. You have to stay inside or have real good rain gear and like the dark.

I like to paint. There's only so much time to put together your life's work, and I'm not getting any younger. So I paint whenever I can.

When I started out, I saw cerebral painters who were running into dead ends. I wanted to think of myself as

Self Portrait without Chocolate Cake and Espresso by Dan DeRoux

serious, but at the same time embracing levity, and in order to keep working I'd draw from all of art history, to patch things together in new ways. A friend of mine calls it "compost-modern." I have always been a convolutionist. Art history, as it turns out, is a never-ending stream of plagiarisms. You'll get in trouble if you do it as a writer or musician, but for some reason painters have always done it.

What does this have to do with living in Alaska? I wrote a little poem about all of this:

I am a painter, not Spaniard but worse.
I paint and I paint for it's that I've been cursed.
I would that I could be a lawyer or saint,
But I have been called to address this complaint.

In Juneau I've lived almost all of my life,
Grew up and married a wonderful wife.
I'd wish it on no one a job such as mine.
Though varied, it's harried, contrived yet sublime.

I stare at a canvas for day after day,
An original thought come my way do I pray.
Sometimes it seems that one may never come
And may never have, but the painting gets done.

Juneau's surrounded by beautiful sights,
Glaciers and mountains and eagles in flight,
But none of this really appeals to me,
It's pretty but give me Duchamp or Magritte.

I love the mixed metaphor, visual puns,
Penguins a-calling upon cloistered nuns,
The Pope as Picasso out catching a fish
In the desert where water is only a wish.

Imagine a city like Venice avail
A whale ashore by means of it's tail.
Or Whistler's mother with teeth so obtruse
A walrus would envy should one become loose

I look out my window and what do I see?
The usual — magnificent scenery.
But close my eyes and what does appear?
The Dutch have arrived and it looks like Vermeer.

These things cross my mind every once in awhile,
And then I commence with a hint of a smile.
I'd like to be serious, heady, profound,
But maybe that waits until next time around.

I try to bring meaning to my living there
In Alaska, I mean, in my traveling chair.
If humor is noble and whimsy all right
I'll get through the gate without having to fight.

Just one more thing that I'd like to say:
If you come to Alaska and don't want to stay,
I'd understand and hope that you'll know
We'd like to go with you whenever you go.

Courtesy of the author

Gregg Erickson lives in Juneau where he has an economic consulting practice and edits the Alaska Budget Report, *a newsletter covering state finances. He has four grown children, none of whom has shown much interest in explosives.*

The Chester Creek Depth Charge

Gregg Erickson

The Concept

When I was fourteen, a schoolmate and I built what would nowadays be described as an "explosive device." We called it a depth charge. We did this in the interest of science, a thirst for adventure, and spurred by a mutual interest in movies depicting submarine warfare in World War II. If we could build a depth charge and make it work, we planned to take a picture of the explosion. In the movies, depth charge explosions produced a two-stage reaction; a heaving up of disturbed water into a sort of dome, followed by a geyser-like plume erupting from the center and shooting maybe fifty feet into the air. We thought it would be pretty photogenic.

We had the perfect place to test our depth charge just a few blocks from our homes in what is now considered downtown Anchorage — the bridge that carried the Alaska Railroad over Chester Creek. Today the creek runs into Bootlegger Cove through a culvert, but in 1955 it was spanned by a timber trestle. There were no fences to prevent access to the tracks or trestle, and my friends and I had often walked across the trestle, and even clambered underneath on the web of lighter timbers that supported the approaches to the main span. As I remember it, the main span was about 75 feet long, underpinned at either end by massive wooden pilings. At low tide the tracks were about 40 feet above mud and rocks, but when the tide came in the water in the center was at least 20 feet deep, and stretched 100 feet or so from bank to bank, fully submerging the bases of the main pilings.

Financing our experiment would be no problem. I was a paper boy for the *Anchorage Times* and had the best route in Anchorage — more than 200 customers in mostly high-density project housing and large apartments, including what is now called Inlet Towers. I could whip through that route in just under one hour, for which, counting tips, I received $110 every month. In 1955, $110 was enough to cover the monthly rent on an upscale one-bedroom apartment.

I'd been carrying papers since I was eleven. Much of my earnings had been put away for college, but I still had plenty to spend. My friend, who I won't name, was similarly well off, as were most kids our age who were willing and able to work in an economy where wages were high and labor short.

The Design

Our depth charge, though constructed from readily available materials, was carefully designed. The explosive was to be contained in a gallon mayonnaise jar. This would sit inside a steel can that had been used to ship powdered milk. I don't remember how big the can was, but it must have held about three gallons. Wet sand was to be packed around the jar to make sure it sank, and to keep the jar from breaking when it hit the water.

Now you would normally think our biggest design challenge would have been figuring out how to get the depth charge to detonate underwater, but in fact, this was the easy part. My friend, whose family was involved in mining, actually had a length of underwater dynamite fuse, the kind that you lit with a match. It made neat sparks as it burned, sort of like a yellow sparkler.

Keeping the water out was the real challenge. We could seal around the fuse where it entered the jar through a small hole in the lid, but what would keep water from squirting in and soaking the explosive powder after the fuse burned past the lid? I don't want someone to use our design to build a modern version of the Chester Creek depth charge, so I will not reveal my clever way around the sealing problem.

The bang in our depth charge came from cherry bombs, large firecrackers — bigger than a cherry, really — with a fuse sticking out like a stem. We would purchase these from a fireworks stand in Spenard. Anchorage city fathers had banned the sale of fireworks, but free-wheeling Spenard was beyond their reach. We would empty the powder from each cherry bomb until our gallon jar was filled with the black, gritty explosive. Easy.

The Logistics

It took way more cherry bombs than we had imagined. Each cost twenty-five cents, and we ended up spending about ninety dollars on them. Lots more trips on our bikes to Spenard than we had planned.

Removing the powder from the cherry bombs was a laborious process. My friend and I each worked on the project at our respective homes. The disused coal bin in the basement at 833 Thirteenth Avenue, where my family lived, was my manufacturing center. When we first moved to Alaska in

1951, our house had a coal furnace with a device called a stoker, an auger-like machine that was supposed to automatically deliver the coal to the firebox. Everyone in my family hated that stoker. Dad finally had it replaced with an oil burner, but the coal bin remained, a small room about six feet by six feet in the corner of our basement, with enough remnant coal under which to conceal the mayonnaise jar as I filled it with the black powder.

Although we started the project with what seemed like plenty of fuse, we used up quite a lot in testing our various sealing schemes. Then I had to snip off another piece to determine exactly how fast the fuse would burn. Using the result of that test, I calculated the length of fuse we would need for our depth charge.

I figured we needed two minutes to drop the depth charge off the trestle, for it to sink to the bottom, and for us to get off the trestle ourselves and to the camera, which would already be set up a little way down the gravel embankment. Adding another minute for "safety," we would need a total burn time of three minutes. By my calculations, the length of fuse we had remaining would consume itself in just over fifty seconds. Crisis.

My friend saved the day. "Lets go down to Northern Supply, and buy some," he suggested. That's exactly what we did. Northern Supply, serving miners (and, as it turned out, minors), was located down in the rail yards, a fair ways by bike, but not too far. The clerk didn't seem to find it at all unusual for a kid clutching a short length of dynamite fuse to be asking to buy more of the same; we paid cash.

Sometime shortly after the Fourth of July, our depth charge was ready to test, but we had to wait a couple of weeks until a high tide coincided with the early morning on a Sunday. There was little chance of a train during the early morning hours, and my friend worked Monday through Saturday, so wasn't easily available on weekdays.

Getting the depth charge down to Bootlegger Cove was difficult. The milk can with its infernal contents now weighed a lot, maybe thirty pounds. Somehow, when my folks were weren't home, I got the thing out of the house and stashed it nearby. My friend spent the night, and under some forgotten pretext we let the family know we would be leaving early. I think we set the alarm for 4:30 A.M. I recall that my Dad came downstairs and offered to make us breakfast. We politely declined, being too much in a hurry.

It was a stunning morning, with bright sun, no clouds, and no wind. We had the streets to ourselves as we tried to carry the depth charge dangling from the middle of a broom stick slung between the handlebars of our two bikes. Somewhere around Eleventh Avenue and L Street, after a couple of crashes, we gave up on this method and lashed the bomb to the rack behind my seat. That was hardly any better, but somehow we made our way west on the gravel of Eleventh Avenue, and coasted down to the sea.

The Test

My friend was in charge of the photographs. He set his camera up on its little tripod, and after a few final adjustments, the two of us lugged the depth charge to the center of the trestle. I looked at my Bulova watch (a prize for being that year's "outstanding junior high school graduate"), and waited until the hands were exactly at 5:55 A.M., the predicted time of high tide. When the second hand went straight up, my shaking hands struck a match and touched it to the fuse. My friend, who was sitting, pushed his feet against the depth charge, and over it went. Before it hit the water we were moving as fast as we could to get off that trestle.

The can sank immediately, oriented as we expected. We waited as the seconds ticked by, one pair of eyes mostly on the watch, the other glued to the barely visible spot where bubbles disturbed the water's smooth, gray surface.

At 5:58, at the precise moment when detonation should have occurred, I yelled "Now!" The exclamation so startled my friend that he pushed the shutter plunger on the camera's cable release, taking a picture of the placid water. He frantically wound the film to the next exposure. He needn't have hurried, because several more minutes elapsed with no sign of anything happening, excepting the faint, faint indication of bubbles.

I have experienced many disappointments since that day, but none affected me as viscerally as the dawning comprehension that our depth charge was a dud. I didn't cry, but I truly felt sick to my stomach. We returned to the trestle, and from the launch point took a closer look. The bubbles were still there, but nothing else. We peered over the edge and exchanged recriminations about what had gone wrong. We had several theories. As it turned out, none was even close.

At about 6:10, as we lay prone on the ties looking down into the silt-filled water, the depth charge exploded with a rumble. For an instant it sounded like a train had materialized out of nowhere and was about to run us down. The entire trestle moved ponderously toward the mountains and then back toward the cove. Rigid with fear, our fourteen-year-old bodies moved with it, held in place by the seaward rail running beneath our bellies. The water below us heaved upward, but there was no geyser-like plume. Instead, a big bubble popped to the surface, with lots of roiling water behind it. A dead salmon appeared and slowly floated out into the cove.

Afterword

Of events that happened that day after the salmon floated away I have no memory. The following summer the Alaska Railroad replaced the Chester Creek trestle, installing a culvert in its place. I did not consider it prudent to inquire about the project, and to this day do not know if it was connected in any way with our experiment. Soon after, though, the railroad erected fences closing off access to that part of their right-of-way.

Why was the detonation delayed? Almost certainly because I had timed the fuse in air; as we later verified, underwater dynamite fuse burns a lot slower under water.

My experiments with explosives continued for two more years, until July 1957. From an abandoned mine in the Talkeetna Mountains I had acquired a coffee can full of blasting caps. While extracting the fulminate of mercury from a cap's innards, it detonated, removing the tips of the first three digits from my left hand. I had been sitting at home on the back steps.

Fortunately, Dr. William Mills, the town's only orthopedic surgeon, had gained lots of experience with explosion wounds as an army doctor in Korea. He repaired my hand pretty well.

"You might want to look around," Mills told my parents. "Those fingers may be out there somewhere."

Sure enough, Mom later discovered the tip of my middle finger in her geraniums. My parents made me pay the medical bills out of my own money, more than $1,000. I gave up on explosives after that, and took up mountain climbing.

David Sheakley

Bridget Smith lives with her husband and two daughters in Juneau.

Riding the Alaska Ferries

Bridget Smith

Most people would consider climbing Denali the peak Alaskan experience, but here's a well-kept secret: Riding the ferry is. So few places exist where we can live fully in the present. An Alaskan ferry is one of those places.

From afar, the blue-and-white ferries may look like cruise ships, but they are not. They are a special form of public transportation on which all classes of people, most of them Alaskans, travel together. There is a casual democracy on the ferry. People routinely sleep on the floor and bring food on board and set up tents outside on the decks. As with the Greyhound bus in other places, the ferry is an essential part of public transportation in Alaska. Like trucks down south, the ferries also transport necessary goods to coastal communities. The ferries, operated by the state of Alaska, run on a marine highway rather than an asphalt one.

The best part about being on the ferry is just that: BEING. It is blissfully easy on the ferry to exist in the present. Point of fact: I have never seen a cell phone used on a ferry. No one has an appointment. No one is rushing off to an important meeting. No one is channel surfing the TV. No one is checking e-mail. No one is running to answer the phone. In fact, no phones ring at all. There is no agenda, no tight schedule, no task to complete, and no "to do" list pending. Without the busy nonsense that characterizes our lives, passengers are free to be. The ferries cruise slowly through the green water, barely even leaving a wake. For people who want to get somewhere quickly, this mode of transportation does not work. It's like life — you are not in control because someone else is at the helm. Your job is to enjoy the ride. The greatest gift of the ferry is that it offers the NOW. More than anything, it is an out-of-time experience, bounded only by arrival and departure.

Most of the trips our family makes are from Juneau north to Haines, where we have a cabin. Alaskans don't measure distance by miles, but by time spent traveling. I couldn't tell you how many miles it is to Haines. The journey takes four-and-a-half hours, enough time to lounge in the solarium watching other people, to stand outside on the deck while mountains and water, fishing boats, and the occasional dolphin and whale roll by. I even saw a deer swimming once. It is time enough to sit in the cafeteria and eat greasy French fries with my daughters, who love "ferry food." It is time enough to sleep, write letters, take a shower, and gab with friends and relatives.

The contented feeling of being in the now starts only when our family actually is on board the ferry. Before that, we pack our car until it can't hold any more and then race out to the ferry terminal two hours ahead of departure time to line up. We hate this part. We don't know why we have to show up two hours ahead of time, but we are afraid that we will get bumped if we don't. As the ferry runs twenty-four hours a day, this means that, theoretically, we can be aboard it at any hour. Although it can't be true, it seems as though departures and arrivals are always in the wee hours of the morning. The truth is that the ferry runs on eternal time, the schedule dictated by the rise and fall of the tides.

Arriving at the ferry terminal is actually the first shifting of gears to SLOW. Ferry terminals are like airports used to be down south. They are small enough so that you can still see everyone who just got off the boat and watch everyone getting on. We sit in our car with the engine off, usually cold, bundled up, drinking out of a thermos, reading, and looking around at the other people in their cars. Many of our cars resemble a scene out of *The Grapes of Wrath* because of the quantities of stuff we've tied to the outsides. We don't dare go to the bathroom because, at any moment, a member of the crew might wave a hand to signal our line to get on.

Meanwhile, we watch as everybody else gets on before we do — the containers, the huge RVs, plus all of the cars and motorcycles and bicycles. We wonder how they are going to cram all of us in. We practice patience. We eye the RVs. Some of them are the size of buses. Some of them are buses, filled with people from far away. If they get on before us, we gnash our teeth, thinking about the sleeping spaces that are rapidly disappearing. Because we frequently sleep on the ferry, we have a vested interest. Sometimes I wonder why there isn't one big dorm some-where on the ship where we can all go to sleep on bunks. As it is, all of the passengers without staterooms sleep together on the floor. I never get on the ferry without my Therm-a-Rest, my sleeping bag, a towel, a toothbrush, a deck of cards, and a good book.

Once our family moves forward to go down the ramp into the ferry, we are so grateful that we burble happily to the purser, who checks our tickets and asks us how we are. Ferry personnel are usually cheery and friendly and helpful. Except for the ones on the car deck. I think they are much more serious because while they are guiding each vehicle in and making sure that we are squeezed in tighter than spawning salmon in a little creek, they are also getting asphyxiated by the fumes from the engines.

After we park on the dark car deck and set our brake, we are officially freed from the bonds of time. Our next task is to try to get out of the car, and sometimes it takes the flexibility of a circus contortionist. Then we walk sideways between the RVs and containers, ducking under the mirrors that stick out. The stairs that lead up to the passenger decks are steep, but we rarely take the elevator, no matter what we're carrying. I guess it is misplaced pride. Our young adult children remind us that the elevator is only for those who really need it. Upstairs, we head to our favorite hangouts. We hardly ever go into the forward lounge of any of the ships except the *Columbia* and the *Kennicott*. It is just not very cozy on the other ships. Once we get settled together, we immediately move off to explore our surroundings. We want to see who's on, what's for dinner, when the gift shop closes, and if the solarium (the covered outdoor area) is packed.

I have a confession to make here. At this point, we are breaking one of the few rules on the ferry: No saving of seats. This is a rule that makes a great deal of sense when the ship is very crowded but it doesn't at other times. It is a rule that also runs contrary to the instinctive behavior of humans. People claim territory that they want to keep for the whole trip and they mark it with their gear. No one wants to find another seat after every bathroom trip. I was on one ship where a territorial claim led to a fist fight — not surprisingly, it was in the middle of the night right after the bar had closed. You can learn a great deal about human behavior on a crowded ferry, especially at night.

Fist fights notwithstanding, Alaskan ferries encourage bonding in a way that other modes of transportation do not. Part of it must be the ship's shape, roundish and big enough to walk around on. The internal design helps, too. Every ferry harbors homey little nooks. We all become a temporary community while we are on board. This sure doesn't happen on a train. The only time I felt part of a community on a train was in Spain when I was the only one with a corkscrew. And in Alaska, with a small population, the recognition factor is high; just as you always know someone on Alaska Airlines, you always know someone on the ferry.

When I take a stroll on the ferry, the most frequent sight I see is people enjoying one another's company.

Families lounge together, classmates read together, couples eat together, teammates talk together and young children play together. The last time we traveled from Haines, our extended family played a cutthroat game of hearts for hours in the cafeteria, happily keeping score on napkins. People discover the abundant entertainment value of other people when they have the time to do so. To my mind, people discover what is important.

The ferry system has been operating for thirty-seven years. And I have had the privilege of riding for thirty-two years. I have ridden the ferry dozens of times. I have been on the ferry with my daughter's third-grade class, with the basketball team from Wrangell, with the high school band from Sitka, with my relatives, by myself, with my women friends, with other writers, with my husband, with my daughters, with my neighbors, with countless tourists from all over the world — back-packers, car campers, RVers, and elder hostellers. And the experience has always been a mixture of humdrum and adventure, a sort of floating summer camp with the ferry personnel acting as camp counselors who aren't too rigid about their campers' behavior. On one memorable trip with a rowdy bunch of women friends, I remember a very polite purser. We were singing our hearts out late at night on the deck because the stars were actually visible. He asked us to keep it down, as some of the other passengers in the solarium didn't realize that stars are a rare sight in southeast Alaska and they wanted to sleep.

What I like most about the ferries — unlike my

children, it is definitely not the food — is the timelessness. It is one of the few places left where a person can just be and feel part of eternity. The mountains have been here for eons, as have the waters and all of the sea creatures and the birds. As we cruise through, we feel calm and a part of all that is.

David Lombardo

Janice (Engstrom) Ryan was born in Nome and lives and works in Anchorage.

I See Camp

Janice Ryan

I grew up in northwest Alaska in the mining town of Nome, a collection of about 3,500 people where the hopeful still prospect on the beach and the only means of joining urban reality is air transportation. Summers were spent at Basin Creek, our (mostly) operating placer mine fifteen miles north of town. Those summers left an indelible mark on our family.

The Nome-Taylor Highway, known locally as the Kougarok Road, is eighty miles of gravel that stretch north from the beaches along the Nome River toward the Sawtooth Range and the Imuruk Basin of the Seward Peninsula. The terrain goes from treeless and flat near the coast to treeless and "mountainous" farther inland. What passes for mountains here are of modest elevation — the highest being Mount Osborn at 4,700 feet — and are old enough to have had most of the dirt and vegetation melt toward the valley floor. The landscape is a beautiful study in subtle color shadings. Deep gray, shale-topped peaks with seemingly permanent pockets of white snow meld into purple and evergreen lichen and tundra just above treeline. About two-thirds of the way down, the willows and alders begin and, depending on the time of year, the colors brighten to reds, golds and oranges. Our version of fall is mid-August to late September, when the colors blaze brighter than one would imagine possible in the Arctic.

Before Dad built the house in town in 1968, we lived at camp as much of the year as possible — usually late May to late September or early October. The road from town inevitably washed out in several places. Luckily, the family vehicle (first an old Chevy Greenbriar van, then a 1969 Chevy C-20 pickup) could usually make it through the washouts and get us back and forth without incident. One fall, we waited overly long to move. The first real snowstorm came in October and the van got stuck about eight miles from town. At three years old, I knew I had to help Dad as he walked to town to recruit someone to pull us out. He, likewise, knew that I wouldn't last twenty minutes. He was right and he carried me, cozy warm and sleeping soundly, into town.

In early May, my parents would begin taking us kids to see how far we could get out the road toward camp. Crammed into the cab of the truck (it was still cold), we had a contest to be the first to spy the one-story buildings that made up the mine. "I see camp!" was the call that announced summer. Our three-room cabin, with out-house, was up on the hill facing south, overlooking the valley and the tailing pile-lined creek below. My grand-parents' cabin, built from an old Army KD (knock down) building, was on the town side of the creek. The bucketline dredge — a three-story structure that floated on a thirty-foot by sixty-foot steel hull with eighteen pontoons — was up the valley toward the watershed.

My grandparents, Herb and Elsie Engstrom, mined up and down the Nome River valley with their three children for several seasons before settling at Basin Creek in 1940. In 1937, they were wintering in Nome when my father, Ron, was born. Beginning in 1938, when Grandpa Herb had sold the house in Nome to finance a season mining at Coffee Creek and lost everything, they traveled Outside in the fall to spend winters in Seattle, a common practice then. At Basin Creek, grandpa used old tractors and a sluice box to mine, before buying the dredge in 1959. Grandpa, Dad and three other local men moved the dredge from Pajara Creek fifty miles west to Basin Creek, using skids pulled by tractors when the ground was frozen and therefore more passable. Thinking of it today, the feat seems nearly impossible, but there the dredge still sits as evidence.

During the late 1960s and early 1970s, the dredge became more visitor attraction than active mine. In fact, a devastating storm left the dredge underwater for part of that time. As a result, in 1966 my grandparents signed a deal with Alaska Airlines and became part of a tour package that brought as many as 180 tourists a day to Nome. Beginning in late-May and continuing through August, visitors would arrive for an overnight stay, with a stop at Basin Creek, followed by visits to other sites in town. The tours continued until 1974 and proved to be one of the formative experiences of my life.

Every day, all summer long, the first bus arrived about

10 A.M. (Because the buses were painted white and the tourists wore pastel parkas, the combination reminded us local kids of Easter egg baskets.) Most often driven by a colorful fellow nicknamed Blueberry John, the travelers made their way over Anvil Mountain, past Dexter Roadhouse, across the Nome River bridge at mile 13 and up the road to Basin Creek. My grandfather's penchant for tinkering and invention, and pure packrat nature, made simply driving our road an experience. Every piece of equipment he'd ever bought, or otherwise acquired, was still present in some form.

Once the bus reached the cabin, Grandpa Herb, Grandma Elsie, and at least two of us kids would board and the storytelling would commence. Grandpa talked of making his way west from Wisconsin, of being put out of business selling Model Ts when the Model A was introduced. Of getting fed up with his skinflint boss in San Francisco in 1932 and borrowing two bits: "Heads I go to Nome, tails I go to Fairbanks!" The outcome of the toss was obvious.

He told of meeting my grandmother, fresh off the boat from Sweden, in Proctor, Minnesota, where she was working in a coffee shop: "Green as the grass, she was, green as the grass." When they met in 1925, Helga "Elsie" Granstrom didn't speak a word of English and my grandfather, at thirty-four much older than she, took full advantage of his parents' native Swedish to win her over. (They'd been married nearly sixty years when he died in 1986. She died the following year.)

On the bus, Grandma would twinkle and blush, a postcard picture of the Swedish grandmother/sourdough's wife. We kids would mingle shyly with visitors, who often spoke no English at all, using the international language of smiles and mutual curiosity that crosses all borders.

Then it was time to proceed up to "the cut," vernacular for where the actual mining took place, so our guests could learn to pan for gold and take their turn at striking it rich. By the late 1960s, wear, weather, and economic reality had conspired to render the dredge temporarily inoperable. Nonetheless, my father would emerge to greet our visitors in his greasy coveralls and explain the workings of this strange contraption.

Dad would describe damming the creek to create the pond and floating the dredge, which used a winch and pulley system, anchored to the relics of past equipment surrounding the pond, to maneuver backward and forward, side to side. He talked about the two-cubic-yard dredge buckets that scooped up material from just above bedrock and hauled it to the third, and top, story of the dredge. Once there, the material was washed through a series of tumblers with increasingly fine screens, the rocks carried away on a conveyor belt, leaving a trail of tailing piles behind the dredge. He explained that the fines were washed down the sluicebox to be collected periodically during clean up. The precious concentrates were dried on the stove in big gold pans; once dry, the black sand and iron pyrite were painstakingly separated from the fine gold and nuggets. The process took a patient hand and so the work was often left to my grandmother, and later my mother, Lorena. They first used magnets, then open-ended, triangular, tin trays that they shook gently while blowing the sand out the end. (Grandma's years of hard work were recognized in 1984, when she was named Alaska's Woman in Mining.)

Once at the cut, Grandma would explain her gold panning technique in her still-strong Swedish accent, demonstrating while bent over the cold water in her Bean boots, Scandinavian wool sweater and bandanna. Lesson complete, visitors would rush the creek while Grandpa, the bus driver, and we kids would disperse and begin giving pointers. "See? You move it in a circle. Be careful not to slosh — you'll get wet. Here, let me show you." The work made for cold hands and feet but our dogs, Pojken and Flicka, helped by nosing the visitors a warm welcome. When everyone was either cold or wet or both (our Arctic summer weather's reputation as inclement being well deserved), we'd head back down to the cabin for refreshments.

The original cabin had been transformed in 1963 by the addition of "the back room." Dad had welded two fifty-five-gallon drums together, in time-honored Bush fashion, to form a stove that heated the large room, and even some of the smaller portion of the house where Grandma and Grandpa lived. Our guests were allowed to thaw by the stove and gaze out the big picture windows while enjoying coffee, tea, and cakes and donuts made by Grandma Elsie, my mother, and my sisters, Linda and Cheryl.

The entertainment didn't stop there. For the remainder of the brief visit, Grandpa Herb would regale them with more stories of life on the Last Frontier. He played several self-taught songs on the pipe organ from a local church he had rescued from the dump and powered with a reversed vacuum cleaner, made all the more melodic by the missing third and fourth fingers on his left hand. After signing the guest book, using the outhouse and perhaps purchasing a postcard or railroad spike (often painted gold by yours truly and my sister, Ronna), our new friends climbed back onto the bus and headed south. Sometimes, we were allowed to ride the bus to town to play with our friends who were not required to "work" as we were, for which we were very envious.

I joke today about having taught thousands of foreign tourists how to pan for gold before I was ten, but I don't think it's an exaggeration: I tried to do the math recently and our total visitor count could have been as high as fifty thousand people.

Life progressed. The tours ended in 1974. By 1980, Dad had the dredge operating again, just in time for my departure to college. I moved from Nome to Marin County, California, at eighteen and discovered the world. My fellow students, many of whom were there to become certified in the English language, simply treated me as though I were another foreign student who happened to be an American citizen. ("Your English is so good!") That acceptance probably helped me combat the culture shock and finish my degree.

I moved back to Alaska in the mid-1980s and have been in Anchorage ever since. I've learned over the years that no matter where you are, whether it's greeting visitors here in "Alaska's largest village" or traveling Outside, Alaska holds an inexplicable mystery and romance that never fails to spark intense interest. Complete strangers are fascinated by stories of the most mundane occurrences.

When the outhouse blew over. When we got stuck crossing the river coming back from berry picking. Or when the grizzly cub climbed on the hot-tub cover at camp, fell in and fouled the water (and later had to be destroyed by the Alaska State Troopers). Or even of learning to drive on the gravel roads of Nome and then learning to parallel park in downtown San Francisco.

It's funny. As a child, it never occurred to me that our life was unusual, that perhaps not every household had hundreds of strangers visit every day. I guess that's why, as an adult, I hesitated to talk about the experience. It just sounded so incredible. But to me it wasn't, so seeing it through others' eyes was more than a little unnerving. That was just what we did, every day, every summer — no matter how out of the ordinary.

Today, in my mid-30s, I'm better at ignoring the self-consciousness this interest generates — it's just life as I remember it — and have become quite good at telling the story. It gives me comfort to remember the birds singing in the morning before the first bus in June, swinging on our swing set in my pajamas. Or hiking up to the waterfall above the dredge with my sister and just listening to the water. Or watching the swallows wing expertly through the air before ducking into Grandpa's shop to nest. Basin Creek is a million experiences that no one else but us enjoyed, growing up as we did in that magical place. And it's mine to treasure when I have a spare moment in my busy adult life. I feel as though I carry a gift with me, ready whenever I need the cheering up.

Through all the years I've lived here, I have never ceased to be amazed at the splendor of our Alaska. With each change of season, I continue to be surprised when the snow creeps down the mountains or when, magically, it's summer and you don't have to wear a coat. Even in January, when I begin longing for the beach or even just the sun, it's easy to remember the things that keep me here. And it's simple. Alaska is my home and I am grateful for it. 🪶

Eric Engman

Diana Campbell lives in Fairbanks with her husband and three daughters.

A New Winter

Diana Campbell

I stepped off the airplane and smack into a wall of hot, wet air. I was confused for a moment, because the wall seemed to wrap itself around me and become an extra layer of clothing. Which I didn't need, since it had to be 100 degrees. Nothing like the extremely cold temperatures I was used to.

The air had a oily feel to it. I wanted to wash my face and hands because my skin felt heavy with grime.

I'd just flown from Fairbanks, Alaska, to Baltimore, Maryland, and it was the first time I'd ever left my small community. I was eight years old that fall of 1967. After a summer of rain in interior Alaska, the swollen waters of the Chena River had picked my family up and dumped us off in my father's country.

The flood presented a good opportunity to go home, my dad reasoned. We had lost most of our possessions and, since we only rented an apartment, we didn't have a house to clean and repair like most people affected by the flood.

So we boarded a series of airplanes and flew across America. From my window seat, I watched massive farmlands and cities pass below.

I had never been on a jetliner before. The only plane I'd every flown on was one of the small bush planes Alaska had plenty of. On that flight, I had watched moose lope through the wild, scrubby land of the Tanana Flats. Only an occasional trail suggested the presence of humans, a trail that seemed to have been built by determination, cut through the stands of willow, spruce, and birch. A lake or pond always appeared at the end of a one of those trails, it seemed.

But the miles of development I viewed as we flew toward our new home suggested organization on a higher level, one I was not familiar with.

My mother, who was half Athabaskan and half Alutiiq, had never been out of Alaska, and neither had my two younger brothers. My father had more of a history of travel. He'd left Maryland with the United States Air Force, which brought him to Eielson Air Force Base, near Fairbanks, in the 1950s.

My mother was a quiet woman, a trait I suspect was brought about by the death of her father when she was very young, and years of Alaska Native boarding schools.

Dad said he loved my mother the first time he saw her. Dad played guitar in a fifties rock 'n' roll band with other GIs, and would drive weekly to Fairbanks to play in a log-cabin burger joint near the University of Alaska. College students came down from the hill the university sat on and pushed the tables and chairs away to dance. My mother was one of them.

Dad pursued her, even selling his guitar for gas money. My father discharged from the Air Force and my parents made a home in Fairbanks. Dad hadn't been back to Maryland since.

Standing on the runway at the Baltimore airport, my mother and her three half-Native children looked to Dad to lead the way to Darlington, his hometown. We piled into a rented car and drove several hours to meet my grandmother, aunts, uncles and cousins. I had no idea what to expect because we had never seen even a photo of them. My father didn't let them know we were coming. My mother was nervous, I could tell.

She had met my grandmother, Mom-Mom, once. My mother contracted tuberculosis when my brother was a baby and I was a toddler. She had to leave Fairbanks to seek treatment in a Sitka sanitarium. My grandmother came to take care of us. I didn't remember her. I only knew her by the boxes of goodies that had arrived regularly in the mail.

Since my mother's relatives didn't live in Fairbanks, we saw them infrequently for short visits. My Alutiiq grandmother, a tiny whirlwind of a woman, taught elementary school in Kotzebue. She lived there with her second husband and their seven children. Other aunts and uncles lived in other communities and we didn't see them much either. But they were all dark-haired and dark-skinned.

We arrived at my Maryland grandmother's home, and after many hugs and phone calls, we were settled into a motel. It was still hot and my father turned on the air conditioner, a contraption I had never seen before.

We went to bed, covered with only a sheet. The room

was pitch black, as was the night. The Fairbanks we'd left had been just starting to get noticeable darkness. Although we were tired, we couldn't sleep because of the crickets. I was used to mosquitoes buzzing around my ears, but there seemed to be an army of creatures outside our door. Horrified as I was to learn from my parents that crickets were some type of bug, I still went to the window to discover what was making the racket. Fireflies floated delicately, like sparks from a fire. The cricket chirping was louder but I couldn't see them. I tried not to be too frightened and forced myself to sleep.

The next few weeks were full of dinners and visits with more relatives.

"Look at how tall the kids are!" my aunts and uncles would say. My dad would puff up and explain it was from eating moose meat and salmon. We would nod in agreement.

My fair-skinned cousins took my brothers and me around to familiarize us with the layout of the land.

"This is dirt. These are flowers," they pointed out to us. My brother and I looked at each other.

"Yeah, we know. We have this stuff in Alaska," we said. I explained how bluebells and fireweed made good decorations on mud pies and cakes.

Darlington was a blink of a town with one main road, but its history went back to the American Revolution. One of my aunts lived in a Revolutionary-period home. The stone Presbyterian church my relatives took us to was just as old, covered with ivy.

The only green things I saw growing on buildings in Fairbanks were the grasses and wildflowers growing on the sod roofs of log cabins. I certainly couldn't point to any structure in my memory that was more than seventy-five years old.

My parents found a place to live and my father went to work. Mom, who had always worked, could not find a job, even with her sterling letter of recommendation and a couple of years of college. She stayed home and read a lot, and took care of my baby brother.

My other brother and I enrolled in the school my father had gone to. I was in fourth grade, and we would study state history, the teacher said.

I explained to my teacher that I had already learned about the reason for Alaska Day and how Benny Benson, a Native boy, had designed the state flag.

"Eight stars of gold on a field of blue," I said.

Well, now I was going to learn about Maryland history, she said. And I did, not only about Maryland but about the history of the original 13 colonies. Our class took field trips to historic places, such as the birthplace of Betsy Ross or Fort McHenry, where Francis Scott Key, aboard a ship offshore, watched "the rockets' red glare" and wrote the national anthem.

Once my mother came on a field trip, this one to Pennsylvania to see Longwood Gardens. It was raining that day so we had to go see the exotic plants in the greenhouse as big as the court building back home. My mother was amazed.

In Fairbanks, she would take my brothers and me for walks in the woods surrounding our apartment. We would wander among the tall birch, spruce, and cottonwood trees, picking flowers, watching small animals, or looking for a future berry patch. We'd stop under a tree to rest and eat the snacks we'd brought. Sometimes we would discover a patch of cranberries or wildflowers, With enthusiasm my brothers and I would dive in, picking to our hearts' content.

"Don't pick all the berries or all the flowers. Leave enough for other people that visit after us," my mother would say. "Also we need to leave enough for the plants to renew themselves next year."

"It's our way," she would tell us. "It's the law of the land." She'd get angry if we tried to take too much.

In Maryland, we begged our mother to take us for a walk like those. She was not at all for tromping off into the unknown forest. We'd already seen six-foot-long black snakes, and even though we were told they were not harmful, we were not convinced. Mom was also afraid of running into a skunk, having heard tales of disaster. And poison ivy. We weren't sure what that looked like. None of those things was in Alaska.

Finally, we convinced her. We chose a dirt road. The road didn't yield anything familiar — not an interesting flower patch or wild berries. In fact, the trees crowded out the sunlight and the woods were full of dark shadows. But they did have a creek with crawdads in it, which my brother thought were pretty cool. But I think it made my mother think of snakes. We were used to bears and moose, big things that you wouldn't accidentally step on.

I missed picking berries. One of my aunts, who wearied of me talking about it, took my to a friend's house.

She had a grape arbor, with fat grape bunches hanging from the vine. They were green and warm from the sun. They were the sweetest things I had ever eaten.

Around Christmas time, it snowed big wet snow-flakes. Barely an inch covered the ground and school was canceled. My brother and I laughed and laughed. They call this snow? But in the summer, when it got dark at night, I'd kept thinking winter was on its way, even though it was 104 degrees.

Try as we did to adjust to strange surroundings, my dad couldn't find steady work, and my mother wasn't happy. It was time to move back to Alaska. My dad went first to find a job and a place to live. In the summer of 1968, after tearful good-byes, we followed.

I looked for the farmland and cities as we headed north. The sky seemed to brighten the closer we got to home.

When I got off the plane in Fairbanks it was near midnight. But it was as light as noon. I was home. ✹

Courtesy of the author

Michael Carey retired as editorial page editor of the
Anchorage Daily News *in December 2000.*

Memo from
Lake Minchumina

Michael Carey

If you roll out a map of Alaska, you will struggle to find the center of the state. The self-proclaimed Last Frontier sprawls from Metlakatla in the rain forests of Southeast to Barrow on the treeless North Slope, and then south past Anchorage and the Alaska Peninsula to the misty Aleutian Islands, which extend far to the westward, toward Asia.

But occasionally you will find a map that comes right out and tells you that the center of Alaska, at least in the minds of map makers, is five miles from Lake Minchumina (pronounced min-chu'-min-ah), just outside the northwest corner of Denali National Park and Preserve. A red dot sometimes marks the spot, with a terse notation testifying to the fact.

Minchumina is the largest of many lakes in the forests that lie between the Alaska Range and the headwaters of the Kuskokwim River to the west. Several writers have pegged the lake at six by eight miles, but the shoreline is uneven, and the lake rambles.

The real estate agent's familiar cry, "Location, location, location," is important to understanding the history of modern habitation around the lake.

Far from the the water highways of the Interior, the Yukon and Tanana rivers, screened by the mountains from development accompanying the Alaska Railroad, Minchumina was as isolated as any place on the map until the airplane became a force.

When adventurer and amateur ethnologist George Byron Gordon of Philadelphia canoed to the lake from Fairbanks in 1907, he met only a handful of Natives and proclaimed the Minchumina area "an uninhabited country."

Geology as much as geography shaped the country Gordon found. The great stimulus to Alaskan exploration and settlement for the first half of the 20th century — gold — was absent. Had a visitor found nuggets in profusion, he would have incited a small army of gold seekers, hundreds of men mucking about the shores of Minchumina.

Native people were not interested in gold. They subsisted on the bounty of the lake and the surrounding hills for thousands of years — fish, moose, fowl, occasional caribou, and the fur-bearing animals. The picture of how they lived is inevitably murky, but they seem to have been nomadic, following their food.

Early in the twentieth century, non-Native visitors reported, the Athabaskans trapped marten, fox and wolf, then mushed through the Kantishna region to Nenana, one hundred fifteen miles to the northeast, or up the Cosna River to Tanana, one hundred miles to the north, to sell their pelts.

In February 1911, when Episcopal priest Hudson Stuck reached Minchumina by dog sled, he found sixteen men, women, and children sharing a large cabin on the west side of the lake. Measles and diphtheria had killed the rest of the local Native population, Stuck said. The Indians had obtained only a minimal grasp of Christianity from their trading trips to Tanana, but all twelve adults owned alarm clocks, and rose "to the summons of no other time piece. At any rate, the clocks went off at intervals, and the natives arose one by one and seemed hugely to enjoy the clatter." By 1920, the Minchumina Indians, with the exception of a family or two, had moved on or succumbed to disease.

Among the Minchumina Natives and their neighbors, there must have been those who could remember the first white men they had ever seen. Carl Sesui, of the village of Telida to the south, certainly did. They were members of the 1899 Herron expedition, soldiers who had been charged with exploring the region for Uncle Sam, men right out of the Lewis and Clark tradition. After the explorers became disoriented (or maybe just plain lost) and were in danger of starvation, Sesui's family rescued the men and their horses, which Carl called "the white man's dogs." It's a poignant moment, the explorers in need of succor, the Natives quickly providing it, neither party apparently aware of the dimensions of change inevitably following contact.

After 1910 and through World War I, white trappers began to arrive at Minchumina in dribbles. Some were prospectors who found the maze of frozen sloughs, bogs, and rolling black spruce south and east of the lake toward Denali National Park worthless to a gold pan but pay dirt to a marten trap.

Others, like Edward Kammersgard, were Alaska Railroad construction hands who wearied of the pick and shovel. Before leaving the railroad for Minchumina in 1916, Kammersgard remembered as an old man, "I told my crew that trapping and hunting were the best ways to enjoy Alaska." Kammersgard also enjoyed fishing — or at least telling fish stories. He claimed that on July 4, 1925, he caught five hundred pounds of pike and white fish with a rod and spoon. The fishing has never been that good since.

Kammersgard picked the right time to go trapping. Fur prices were strong around World War I and would go higher in the twenties. A large marten or a large lynx brought $30 and a high-quality silver fox brought $500 in those years.

Kenny Granroth followed in Kammergard's footsteps at the end of the Depression. He came as part of a construction crew that built an airport along the shores of the lake. On a clear Minchumina day, Mount McKinley rises from the Alaska Range unobstructed, so brilliantly white and perfectly proportioned that unprepared visitors struggle to believe their eyes. The view is equally spectacular summer or winter. "When I saw that," Granroth recalled, "I put down my duffle bag and said 'This is the place for me. I'm not leaving.'"

Granroth's life paralleled the changes in technology and communication that people around the lake experienced. In late 1941, he went trapping with an old-timer of the Kammersgard generation, Herman Olson, as his partner. When the two returned in the spring of 1942, they were stunned to discover that the Japanese had bombed Pearl Harbor. The two must have been among the last men in North America to get the word.

By the time failing health drove Granroth from the lake in the early eighties, he had television and watched the World Series live.

After World War II, a dozen or so trappers called Minchumina home. My father, Fabian Carey, was one of them.

Fabian bought his trapline from Carl Hult, like Kenny Granroth one of the Minchumina trappers. Hult was in perpetual financial trouble no matter how big his fur catch. He sold a large section of his trapline south of the lake to my father to finance one of his divorces.

"Big dividends, big dividends for both of us," Hult said in a letter to Fabian promoting the sale. In a sense he was right. During the years right after the war, the pent-up demand for consumer goods pushed fur prices so high that trappers were later to think of this period as the Golden Age. Trappers who operated out of Minchumina considered 100 marten in the seventy-six-day season a good performance. During his first season, 1946-47, Fabian caught only 45 marten, but two years later he took 150. A trapper could earn $4,000 in a winter. Not bad in an era when the dollar was worth seven times more than today, and a new Levittown home near New York City cost less than $8,000.

A Minchumina trapper worked hard for his money, routinely encountering snowed-in traps, drifted trails, and competitors who cut into his profits, from mice that chewed up marten skins to bears that, in their relentless search for food, wrecked trapping cabins. As the 1947 season came to a close, Fabian wrote in his diary, "Went down the creek with dogs and picked up traps — no fur. Plenty chilly yet. Hope this cold spell breaks. 55 below." Such temperatures could last a week or more.

Summer offered plenty of hard work, too. Reliable, lightweight chainsaws had yet to replace muscle power. A day on the woodpile was a day spent as a partner of the Swede saw and the ax.

Gardening called after the ground warmed — planting and cultivating potatoes, beans, spinach, chard, carrots, and turnips to join moose meat and fish on the dinner table. For color, Fabian added nasturtiums, bachelor buttons, and poppies, but most trappers figured the weeds nature provided were decoration enough.

Life at Minchumina, however, was not standing still while the weeds grew in old-timers' yards. In 1939, the Roosevelt administration, wary of the war clouds gathering over Europe, selected eleven Alaska communities for new air fields that would strengthen aviation and transportation on the United States' northern perimeter. Minchumina was not this list, but when the Civil Aeronautics Administration began adding additional sites in 1941, the lake's location, half-way between Fairbanks and McGrath, led planners to conclude it was optimal for providing weather reports and other flight information and would make a good emergency landing site.

Construction crews armed with powerful bulldozers and graders brought overland in the winter came next.

A revolution in travel followed. The 5,000-foot gravelled field cut out of the hillside guaranteed the Minchumina people regularly scheduled air service year around in a fully modern DC-3.

The airplane redefined time and distance for those at Minchumina. "Town," a synonym for Fairbanks, now was merely an hour a way, not days distant as it was behind a dog-team or in a boat. A trapper like Carl Hult could run into Fairbanks on impulse to shop or gamble.

The airfield meant more members of the Minchumina community as the Civil Aeronautics Administration (today the Federal Aviation Administration) sent in technicians to report the weather, take care of the field, and operate communications and navigation equipment. Eventually, the government built a half-dozen suburban, two-story frame homes near the end of the field for the staff. The homes looked as if they had been lifted from an eastern developer's brochure promising the American dream. The incongruity of this enclave, bright red brick chimneys filling the frozen winter air with steady streams of stove oil smoke, was not lost on the aeronautics administration employees and their families. A few of the employees were game enough to buy traplines, but the newcomers were more significant because they expanded the community, providing the trappers with new companions and economic opportunity in the form of occasional day labor. The agency was present for more than twenty years, until the government decided manned facilities were an unnecessary expenditure and closed them all over Bush Alaska.

Today the Lake Minchumina community has perhaps

thirty people in summer, twenty in winter. A few trap, some work at the handsome lodge owned by Jack Hayden, others are retired. Still others take jobs in town for part of the year — or even for years — intending to return. The airplane is still the choice for travel. There is no road outlet. Minchumina remains far too inaccessible and remote to justify the expense of one, although former Gov. Wally Hickel briefly put the area in his expansive road-building plans.

From a canoe in the middle of the lake, the hills to the north and lowlands to the south look much as they did when Hudson Stuck arrived almost a century ago, or on the day Kenny Granroth proclaimed Minchumina the place for him.

The major challenges residents face remain similar, too, despite the arrival of the television, the telephone, and the microwave oven.

• How do you make a living in the Alaska Bush?

• Are you really comfortable with life in the woods, far beyond the rim of modern civilization?

Over the last hundred years, the number of men and women around Lake Minchumina who have answered these questions successfully has been small. My father, for example, realized by 1950 that fur prices would not hold. He also understood that his children needed schooling. So he moved to Fairbanks. Until he died in 1975, Fabian struggled with the question "Do you live in town or do you live in the woods?" This struggle took the form of trapping some winters and staying in Fairbanks to work for wages during others.

I developed an intense personal attachment to

Minchumina as a boy. Our cabin on a hill along the west end of the lake was the first place I recognized as home. To visit Minchumina, as I try to do every summer, is to visit my history and my father's history.

And to see the face of the Alaska wilderness at both its plainest and most beautiful right outside my window. 🦈

Peter Porco

Maeve McCoy is a seventh-grader who enjoys skiing in the winter and bicycling in the summer.

Changing Seasons

By Maeve McCoy

I've lived in Anchorage all my life; twelve-and-one-half years to be exact. I went to Willard Bowman Elementary from kindergarten through sixth grade, and I am currently attending Steller Secondary School.

I've observed a lot of weird weather in my time here. Basically of weather you can experience in Alaska, I've experienced it. I've seen snowstorms in May, thirty-six degrees Fahrenheit in January and an EXTREMELY cold spell (minus twenty-two degrees Fahrenheit) three years ago.

There is one thing about Alaska's weather that I love, though, and that is its seasons. Sure, there are six months of winter, and a mushy, gushy spring, but all the seasons are wonderful in their own way. I'm always either enjoying a season, or anxiously waiting for Mother Nature to hurry up and get to the next season.

There's autumn. I'm in school during this season, so I always associate fall with looking out a school window and seeing the red and gold leaves set against the clear

October sky. There's not a sky like that in any other season, a very clean, deep, pure blue that doesn't exist in a Crayola box. It's like a giant bowl that fits itself over the world. You can see the curve of it. The two colors, reddish and blue, contrast brilliantly and vividly.

Next is winter. There is something truly magical about driving home from Borders on a Friday night with two new books, the car heater on, and everything inside is warm and toasty and you are content. You don't have to get up tomorrow. You can snuggle in bed, staying up late, drinking hot cocoa. You pass light poles, their muted triangles of light displaying the softly fluttering, flittering, flurrying little white snowflakes.

Spring arrives soon. Spring in Alaska involves hearing on the radio how much daylight we've gained, and seeing the tiny green buds on bare trees. It's almost like summer and winter combined. On the ground is wet snow, and in the soft blue sky is a warm yellow sun and white puffy clouds, very unlike the monotonous white sky of winter.

Then, of course, there are the giant, dirt-brown puddles filled with chunks of floating ice — mini Arctic Seas — and there's the combination of water/snow that inhabits parking lots this time of year. You find mittens and earrings and coins and books and dollars alike when the snow melts, earning Alaska spring its nickname: Breakup.

And then there's summer. I never truly appreciated the Alaskan summer until I spent the first three weeks of June in New York. It was never sunny there, only humid and cloudy. Even though I loved the vacation, the weather was a horrific experience. When we got back to Alaska, it was as if I'd died and gone to heaven. The air was cool and calm, the skies were nice and cloudy, and there was a soft breeze. Then there were those days when the sun poured out of the clear blue sky, lighting everything with a soft yellow glow.

If someone asked me to tell him what my favorite season is, it would be whatever season I am in when he asked me. 🏴

Chris Arend

Terzah Tippin Poe was born in Fairbanks and currently lives in Anchorage.

Old Van, Dried Eggs, and Spam

By Terzah Tippin Poe

Every spring, Anchorage, Fairbanks and Juneau swell with people from rural areas, who wake from the hibernation of winter and make their way to the urban centers to celebrate the ritual of shopping. Sort of a summer hunting party, except all the critters are dead and pre-packaged.

And every year I look forward to my father returning to civilization from the wilds of Alaska. After yet another winter of wondering whether Dad made it through the piles of freezing snow and the waking of the bears, he emerged from his cocoon of a cabin in North Excursion Inlet, called me on his cell phone, and announced he was coming in for supplies.

"Terzah, I'm coming to Juneau. *crrrrraaaacccckkkk* …can you hear me? *Hiiiissssss*….be there *crrrrraaaacccckkkk* …9 A.M. nex *hiiiissss* Sunday."

Cell phones are not exactly the most reliable communication devices when you are living two hours from the nearest repeater cell, and towering mountains on three sides hide line-of-sight. Not to mention that Dad has to hike around half the day hunting for a spot that will actually throw a signal out to me — which probably explains why I don't hear from him much during the winter months.

Occasionally, the phone will ring in my warm, cozy, electricity-driven house in Juneau and all I'll hear when I answer is an incredible hissing and cracking noise. I then know my father is still alive and doing well. No words are exchanged, but from the tenor of the hissing I can tell things must be OK.

Now, for Dad, making his way to Juneau is a series of well-thought-out steps, each precariously built on the other, held together with the glue of spring optimism. At the end of journey lie the shining Mecca of Fred Meyer, and the great god of all things good, Costco.

Dad's spring migration begins by cutting a path through mounds of bear scat, wheeling his Jeep down the nine-hundred-foot dirt road to the beach, motoring five miles along the coastline in his skiff, boarding a chartered Cessna 206 at the cannery and flying south to the big city, Juneau, list in hand.

The fun part of such an excursion for me is riding shotgun as we harvest supplies in Juneau. Cranking up the old, rust-colored — not to mention rusted-out — '75 Ford Econoline family van and making the rounds in style. You have to understand, this is not just any old van. My father customized this vehicle long ago. This customizing revolved around ripping out all non-essential interior elements such as passenger seats to maximize carrying capacity, strapping a propane tank to the back, and installing a wood rack on the roof to store the bright red kayak.

This old soul of a vehicle not only serves as my father's urban transportation, but it also has been his constant companion for more than twenty-five years. Long before the move to Excursion, Dad simplified his way of life by divesting himself of almost all worldly possessions — house, furniture, books, etc. — and hit the road. Life became a steady progression of downsizings, from house to small apartment to sailboat.

The old van changed with the times, and evolved from a mere vehicle to a home away from home. Custom wood bunks grew inside and storage systems advanced to a new level of sophistication. Eventually the lure of the wilderness became too much for Dad to resist, and he took to the Alaska highways and lived out of his van-turned-apartment.

No turnout was too small, no road too steep for Dad and van. Although rear wheel drive, the thing performed like a monster four-wheeler — at least in the mind of its driver. Often the pair were spotted careening down the Haines Highway or puttering up the Richardson. Stories would drift back to me of my father and van mysteriously turning up at the oddest places at the oddest times. Fairbanks in winter? Juneau in fall? Haines Junction in spring? Occasionally he would check in and let me know things were hunky-dory, and that he had plans to check out this or that creek rumored to be the mega grayling spot. I never could figure out what the big deal was about grayling, but to my Dad it was the Holy Grail of all fish.

The days of adventure are pretty much over for our

old van; it now lives in semi-retirement in Juneau awaiting Dad's twice yearly visits to the big city. Patient and quietly crumbling from Southeast rust infestation, it usually greets our arrival with just the vaguest murmur of recrimination before roaring to life.

So, as we clamored into the van last spring to scout for food and supplies, Dad and I both felt an exhilarating sense of adventure return. Another road trip! Yes, technically a spin around town in Juneau qualifies as a bona fide road trip; there ain't no way to drive out of this little burg. This was as good as it was gonna get for the three of us, so we made the best of it.

First stop, Fred Meyer. Among other things I have learned from my father is that it's imperative for a person living year-round in the middle of nowhere to acquire as much freeze-dried eggs as possible. Encased in shiny, rain-repellent packages, this powdery substance is the basis for many a hearty meal, not to mention its usefulness as a packing material for the journey back to Excursion. As we walked the aisles of Fred's, Dad extolled the virtues of this protein in a packet.

"Do you know how many different meals can be created from just one of these little guys? I can make a breakfast of eggs and Spam, a lunch of scrambled eggs and catsup, and a dinner of beans and eggs — and still have some left over for a midnight snack."

My father's relationship with freeze-dried eggs is long and enduring. In the sixties and seventies, he swore by them as a crucial component of the many Boy Scout camp outs he lead in both Fairbanks and Juneau, and in the eighties his bond grew deeper as they were the bedrock of his 780-mile hike from Fairbanks to Haines. That thirty-eight-day journey, through every kind of weather and terrain Alaska could throw at him, with a sixty-pound pack on his back, solidified the true value of lightweight, portable protein in a packet. With every step along the way, Dad became intimate with every ounce of weight he was carrying. His measure of what constituted good food became no longer a matter of taste, but rather of weight. The less it weighed the better it tasted.

I guess that philosophy stuck with my father. While most people talk about food in terms of quantity and flavor, my father continues to drift back to the weight issue anytime food is mentioned. Most people's concern with food is about gaining weight. My father's is about carrying it. Eventually I came to believe that if my Dad had enough freeze-dried eggs he would be good-to-go in any situation, whether living on the road, hiking across Alaska, or holed up in his cabin in the middle of nowhere.

Personally, I find it difficult to gauge just how much freeze-dried eggs one person requires in a year, but the forty or so packets Dad grabbed off the shelves just didn't seem to provide the necessary bulk a grown man needed to fend off the elements for any length of time. I was skeptical of my father's assertion that this was plenty of eggs to get him through the winter. Heck, if forty packets was good, then forty more would be even better. Who knew whether he would be able to get out of Excursion before break-up, and a guy could really be hurting for protein by that time. So, I flagged an unsuspecting stock boy and asked him to check in back for more of the precious substance.

"How many do you need?" he asked peering down at the mass of shiny protein packets swimming in our cart.

"Well, how many do you have?"

I felt I had entered critical negotiations on behalf of my Dad — who, by the way, had wandered off to check out some fancy new packets of freeze-dried deluxe soups. The outer wrapping of the soups had pictures of hot, steaming liquid and extolled the extraordinary taste sensations waiting to be set free with the addition of a little boiling water. My father's only comment as his picked one up was, "Wow, this is so lightweight and it says it serves four per packet!"

In the meantime, I had brokered a deal with the stock boy; if he went to check on more freeze-dried eggs we would surely buy them. My father returned to the cart and assessed his supplies. "Ya know, I really think that is going to be enough to last me. One person can only eat so many eggs."

I whirled around, surprised. He went on, "I don't think you are calculating the expansion factor into the equation."

It was too late however, as the stock boy had returned bearing a box of freeze-dried eggs. I had made a deal and I was going to stick with it, and my father was going to live with the consequences. After all, freeze-dried eggs don't spoil. Do they?

We loaded Dad's supplies from Fred's into the van and made haste to our next destination, Costco.

We strolled the aisles, admiring the immense vastness of the store's shelves and supplies. You get the sense any-thing is possible in Costco, that if they don't carry it, it must not be necessary to life. It is truly the giver of all things good. And as much as you want.

Now, up to this point we had managed to gather a veritable cornucopia of carbohydrates (not counting, of course, the freeze-dried eggs): cookies, crackers, dried potatoes, rice. I grew concerned that my father was not adequately addressing his nutritional needs. After, all one cannot live on dry foodstuffs alone.

"How about some real, live food Dad? It's not like you will have carry this stuff around on your back for forty days."

My father's face brightened with the possibilities. Although we did have to consider that he hadn't yet worked out a cold storage system capable of handling fresh food, canned goods were definitely manageable. And we were standing in the middle of the Vatican City of bulk canned goods.

We rounded the corner with our flatbed cart, and — lo and behold! — before us stood a mountain of Spam. As my father started fondling the dark blue tins, I could tell he was calculating the amount needed to last the season, and the myriad of possibilities this pseudo-ham-in-a-can provided.

I have always believed that when they designed this particular food item, they had my father in mind. As far back as I can remember Dad has had a can or two of Spam floating around. I would find partially rusted tins stashed in several key locations in the house and garage, adrift in the back of the van, or squirreled away in a corner of the sailboat.

Now, the funny thing is I can't clearly recall ever eating

Spam. I know I must have since I have a pretty good idea what it tastes like — or should I say what it doesn't taste like. I vaguely remember early morning weekend breakfasts with scrambled eggs (real) and some meat that I recognized from its shape must have been Spam. But why buy it now, when there were so many other canned meats to choose from? What was its lure?

I just had to ask.

"Dad, what exactly IS Spam anyway? Isn't it like some kind of unknown meat-stuff? Couldn't you just go with some of the fine new-fangled canned meats like REAL ham instead?"

This line of questioning apparently had the taint of sacrilege, as my father turned his back on me and began to build a pyramid of cans on our cart in homage to this staple of northern life. One thing I did notice is Spam is perfectly designed to stack one on top of another, upper lip of the can embracing the bottom of the one placed on top — the Lego equivalent of food containers. The designers clearly made up the weight disadvantage with the ability to conveniently pack these cans for shipping.

"I don't know what it is about this stuff, but I know I like it," Dad replied as he proudly surveyed his blue-tinned monument.

Yes, it was a monument. A monument to the known, the comfort of the familiar that keeps bringing my father back to this cliché of the north. As strange as it sounds, Spam represents a simpler time when a food's weight wasn't as much of a concern as its ability to feed a family and last the winter. The familiar blue tin brings back memories of life in Alaska in the fifties, when my father first arrived, of the winters in Barrow where he met and married my mother, of the sixties and seventies when our family lived in Fairbanks, and of most of Dad's nomadic years. With all that has changed for my Dad and I, one thing has remained the same — Spam.

Standing on the tarmac at the Juneau airport, we finished loading my father's supplies into the plane for his return home to North Excursion.

"See ya in the fall for Thanksgiving and another whirlwind tour of the town," said Dad as he reached to hug me.

Yeah, I thought, if that old van can just stand up for one more year of harvesting we'll be set. ⚓

Janis Lestenkof

Harley Sundown is a thirty-seven-year-old Yupik high school teacher who was born and raised in Scammon Bay.

My Heritage

Harley Sundown

Before I was born in the early sixties, the Bureau of Indian Affairs ran the schools in most rural Alaska villages. This was the time village Alaska was truly Alaskan. No running water, no electricity, no radio, no TV, and a lot of Yupik language spoken. There were teachers flown in from the Lower 48. Most villages had one- or two-room schools.

There was a teacher/principal living here in Scammon Bay with his family. His name was James; his middle name was Harley. He visited my family while my mom, Mary Ann Sundown, was carrying me. He told my mom to name the baby after him. Shortly after, he was killed. I was born Harley James Sundown. Somehow that principal knew he would not be around. That's how my name came to me.

I grew up in a very traditional family. When I was in my fives, my dad, Teddy Sundown, was at least sixty, my mom in her late forties. My dad followed the traditional cycles of animals. Our whole life revolved around them.

In the spring, he fished for herring. Every spring he would look at the clouds and tell me, "The herring are here." I always tried to copy his observations. After herring fishing, he was the first to set a net in the Kun River in front of the village. He would be the first to catch a chum or a king salmon. He'd make sure everyone got to eat the first fish of the year.

I can still see him today, putting on his *irvuciqs* (waterproof boots made of sealskin). He'd sit on the living room floor, rolling the tundra grass into an oblong shape and inserting it in the boots. He'd wrap a burlap bag or homemade liner on his feet, slip on the boots, take them off again if the grass didn't feel right, adjust the grass and slip the boots back on. He'd be in no hurry.

After this ritual, he'd walk down to the net site. We could see him walking down to the net over the moist, brown tundra, the air full of little birds flying and geese making noise overhead. It would be a nice, sunny morning and we could see his lone silhouette with the blue sea behind him. Sometimes I would go with him and see the oblong print the *irvuciqs* would make in the soft mud. He prided himself on being the first to his net site. At low tide, he'd take the fish from his net and wash them in the river before putting them in the burlap sacks that lay on the bank thirty feet above him. If he caught too many fish, he'd pick the net clean, set the fish on the beach and pick them up with the boat during high tide.

My mom would walk out when the earth turned green to pick *tarnaq* (wild celery). We'd all walk west of the village to a corner of the hills by the ocean. She and my dad would pick an *isgan* (grass bag) full of *tarnaq*.

We'd peel the top layer off and dip the *tarnaq* in a bowl of seal oil and crunch for lunch.

Early every fall, my Dad would cut wood and start shaving foot-and-a-half-long sticks. He'd be in the *qasgiq* (men's bathhouse) sitting on the floor. (The *qasgiq* is still located across from my mom's house.) He'd shave stick after stick of wood and place them in a bundle. I would see the wood shavings fall on the floor in perfect spirals. When he was done, he would stand up and more wood shavings would rain off his pants.

He used the sticks to make *iluuligaqs* (funnels for blackfish traps). He'd get at least ten done every fall. They were always gone as soon as he made them. Men would come to the house and pay him $25 per funnel. I always marveled at his ability to shape the funnels, from approximately a one-foot opening at one end to about a three-inch opening at the other end. This was just enough to let the blackfish pass through to the body of the trap

His next project was making mink traps with chicken wire. He made about fifty mink traps, and then he crushed them so they could fit into the sled. He then waited till freeze-up to set the traps.

As soon as the rivers froze, my dad was one of the first to check the river. He spent every morning observing the skies and the air conditions and looking at the river. He walked down to the river with a small ice pick in his hand. The ice pick was a sensor that fed him data about the water and ice. Ice safety was measured by jabbing. If the ice pick did not penetrate the ice, it was safe to stand on. He stood on the ice and methodically jabbed his way across the river, checking in front of him every few steps. When he finally got to the other side, he came back not using the ice pick as much. He told the rest of the men and the mink-trapping season was open.

In the mornings, my mom's and dad's coffee cups clanked as they mixed sugar and milk with the coffee. I would lie in bed listening as they spoke about that day's plans. My mom made down blankets and they were so warm and homey in the mornings. Made me want to stay in bed all day. The ritual in the morning was to wake up and start a fire in the stove. In the winter, my mom would wake up and the wash basin would be frozen at least half an inch. That's because we only had a wood stove. Dad or Mom would turn on the Blazo lamp and look out the window. Part of looking out the window was to find out the weather and part was to see if our neighbors were up. Every morning by 6 A.M. or 7 A.M. our neighbor's lights were already on. They always seemed to be up before us.

Before 8 A.M., my Dad was hitching up the dogs. As soon as he hitched up the first dogs, the other dogs, sensing something was going on, would scream at the top of their lungs: *aar ra rra rra rra rra rrra*. The whole village seemed to be making noise as almost all the men were hitching up their dogs. It was time to cross the river to the mink and blackfish creeks that filled the whole area north of us. That area is all flat, dotted with lakes, rivers, and narrow sloughs that eventually go out to the ocean. In them swim the six- to eight-inch blackfish that the mink and my family depended on so much to eat.

The dogs were so strong, it was hard to keep them

from running away with the sled. Each dog would leap forward trying to pull the sled. They were very impatient every morning. One day the dogs were so anxious to go they yanked and yanked till the anchor pulled out. My dad chased the sled but could not catch them. Another man put my dad in his sled and caught the dogs.

Mink was very important to our families in the village since they provided good money for food and clothing. Every year dad went up north to the Black River area to sell his furs. He'd come back with flour, sugar, tea, coffee, bullets, shotgun shells. In my grown-up years I went up to Uksuqalleq, an old trading post on the Black River north of the village. I explored the run-down Northern Commercial Company post and found a receipt for my Dad. I thought back on all the hard work he went through to raise nine daughters and one son.

My dad did go through some very tough times along with my mom because, until I came along, they never had any sons. My mom tells me stories about how her sister and brother wanted to trade kids so we could have boys in the family to help our dad. She said, "No way." Kids are very valuable to her. She never ever wanted to give kids away, even though the practice of giving away kids was very common among the older parents. It was a means of providing a much-needed girl or boy to families.

Their oldest daughter, Zita, is in her sixties now and living in Redding, California. She has four kids, two of whom graduated from college. Their second oldest daughter, Theresa, lives here in Scammon Bay. She is in her late fifties and is a cook at the school. Her oldest daughter graduated from college and teaches first grade for our school.

Their next daughter, Modesta, is also in her fifties and is a cook in Bethel. One of her daughters graduated from college and teaches elementary in Bethel. Alice, the fourth daughter, lives in Scammon Bay and is the Yupik teacher for the elementary and high school.

Loddy, the fifth daughter, lives in Bethel and is the head of the Yupik Immersion School there. She got her teaching degree from the university at Fairbanks and has won numerous teaching awards from the state and nationally. Leota is the sixth daughter and she is the head of the preschool program in the village. She got her teaching degree through distance delivery courses from Fairbanks.

Agnes is the seventh daughter. She lives in Bethel with her family She works in one of the elementary schools and she has kids going to college. Dorothy is the eighth daughter and she lives in Colorado with her husband. She got her associate's degree and works as a bank teller. Susan, the ninth daughter, lives with her husband in Scammon Bay.

Myself, I am the youngest and live in Scammon Bay, where I teach in the high school. I was very fortunate to have won the Milken Award, given each year to the top teachers in the United States.

I also have two brothers and a sister adopted into the family. George, who is older than I am, works as the tribal administrator in Scammon Bay. Robert, who is younger, works for the U.S. Fish and Wildlife Service in

Bethel. He got his degree in biology from Fairbanks. Joann, who is the youngest of the sisters, got her teaching degree from Fairbanks and teaches second grade here in Scammon Bay.

I grew up not knowing a word of English. I know my sisters did go to school because they always brought books and work from school. I would watch the Christmas programs the school put on. They would always act out the Nativity scene every year, sing the Christmas songs and give out school presents. I would try my very best to talk like I was putting on the play but my English always came out wrong. I didn't even know whom to call a Mister or Missus correctly.

Loddy loved to read comic books and she would often bring them home on her trips to Scammon. When I first saw Richie Rich, Archie, Donald Duck, Sgt. Rock, Billy the Kid, Jonah Hex, Superman, I fell in love. I couldn't wait till Loddy brought more comics. I would lay on Mom's bed and read while eating bread. I don't ever remember learning to read but the comics were so easy to understand with their color pictures and easy words.

One Christmas, she gave me a huge box of comics for a present and I thought it was the best present I ever got. I lived adventures away from the village every day I could. I went to all the countries the cartoon characters visited, ate the food they ate, and lived in the mansions they did.

I remember going to church every day the Catholic priests were here in the village. I remember my mom and dad devoutly praying in church, eating the body and blood of Christ. (I saw my mom and dad pray every night before they went to bed. My dad always got on his knees in bed with his head almost touching his knees. He was crouched like a ball. The same thing happened when he woke up except he sat up in bed.) I would crawl under the seats and look up at my mom and dad. I would see the Amukons sitting on the other side, my Aunt and Uncle Akerelreas, my Aunt and Uncle Kasayulis, the Ulaks, the Aguchaks and other villagers. This gave me lifelong churchgoing habits I find still important today.

After church on Sundays, we always went to catechism run by the priest. The best part of going to catechism was getting a piece of hard candy. Candy was extremely hard to find in the village since we only got a barge once a year. The store got its supplies by that Bureau of Indian Affairs-run barge. There were hardly any airplanes, since we didn't have a runway in the village then. The few planes that came in were floatplanes in the summer and ski planes in the winter. I don't even remember what the priest taught us except that hard candy tasted so good.

Every Sunday I bring my whole family to church. I know they must be like I was. They must not be paying attention to all the words being spoken in church. My kids are always paying more attention to others as they sit. Sometimes they get so distracted I have to remind them they are in church. The lifelong good habits are being developed as they learn by example.

I have ten very beautiful children that I value so much now. Herschel is my oldest at seventeen, Thea is fifteen, Ekamtalria is thirteen, Canar is eleven, Wybon is nine, Shayna is six, my brat Angel is three, my adopted boy Jerry is two, my boy Theodore, named after my Dad, is one, and my little daughter Misty Blue is four months. Someday, I hope they write about the good memories that shaped their lives as my memories shaped mine. 🪶

Brian O'Donoghue

Kate Ripley lives in Two Rivers with her husband, Brian O'Donoghue, their rowdy young sons, Rory and Robin, a yard full of howling sled dogs, and a patient old cat.

Clear Boundaries

Kate Ripley

Capital movers piss me off.

I used to think no reasonable person of average intelligence could argue in favor of stripping Juneau of its capital city status. It wasn't until I moved from Southeast to the Interior in 1992 that I began to realize the goofy idea actually had widespread support.

I was shocked at the hostility my hometown generated during casual conversation. "They're all capital movers here, Dad," I told my father, Rudy Ripley, a retired sign painter and print shop owner who battled in several capital move fights along with his pals in the Juneau Chamber of Commerce. "Up here, 'Juneau' is a dirty word."

At parties in Fairbanks, my cheeks would flush and my heart would quicken a few beats when the topic came up. Because I was from Juneau, my opinions on the matter were quickly dismissed.

"You're not a real Alaskan, Rip," one friend said. "You're from Juneau, for Christ's sake!"

Never mind that I am a sixth-generation Alaskan.

Never mind that Juneau is a lot closer to "Alaska" than upstate New York, where this friend had come from a few years earlier.

The historian in our family is my great uncle, Robert Fleek. According to his research, my great-great-great grandmother was Maria Aleksandrovno Ol'gin, born in Kodiak in 1848. She married a Maryland-born Irishman, Edward Cashel. Maria and Edward had Sarah, who married a Norwegian named Andrew Berg. Sarah and Andrew had Elizabeth, who married a Pennsylvanian named George Fleek. Elizabeth and George had Marjorie, who married a Douglas-born Finn named Tauno "Tic" Niemi. Marjorie and Tauno had my mom, Judy, who married my dad, who came from Washington state as a young boy. My mom and dad, of course, had me.

Our ancestors lived in Kodiak, Katmai, Unga, Douglas, Chichagof, and Juneau. They were mostly miners and fishermen. My great-great grandparents Sarah and Andrew Berg moved their family to Douglas from Unga in 1900, a trip that took twenty-one days by steamer.

We've been there, and in Juneau, ever since.

A poster of my family tree, labeled "The Amazing Matriarchy," hangs on my living room wall. With the exception of my Grandpa Tic, all of my Alaska lineage was passed down through the women.

In an absurd way I feel as though this heritage gives me automatic bonus points in the capital move debate. As if what I have to say about it is the final word.

Yet the subject is off limits in my own marriage.

My husband, Brian O'Donoghue, is, sadly, a mover.

In most respects, Brian is an extremely intelligent and

talented man. He has his master's degree in journalism. He's traveled the world as a merchant mariner, run both the Iditarod and Yukon Quest one-thousand-mile sled-dog races, and — most impressive — he wired and Sheetrocked our entire house.

But on the capital move, he's just plain stupid.

The main point he and others bring up is access.

Like a lot of other places in Alaska, you have to take a boat or a plane to get to Juneau. State ferries run to Juneau from Skagway or Haines every few days or so. But that's only after someone from Fairbanks or Anchorage — seven hundred to eight hundred miles away — has traveled by car for some sixteen hours. Flights are costly. Even the most direct air routes take half a day. Then there's Juneau's notorious fog, which results in numerous delays or over-flights that land you in Ketchikan or Seattle.

In other words, it's hard to get there. It's an "island" locked within ice fields and glaciers. And that's one reason I love it.

When I was twelve, our family took a big vacation "down south," my term for anything lower than the fifty-eighth parallel. We went to Seattle; Washington, D.C.; Florida; and the Bahamas. As part of the trip, we rented a car and drove from the top of Florida to the bottom.

"Where does one town end and the other begin?" I wondered, loudly, from the back seat. "You can't tell. They all meld together."

I was disturbed. I had grown up taking ferries to Haines, Sitka, and Petersburg. The loudspeaker would blast our arrival, usually at some ungodly hour like 2 A.M. or 4 A.M. Nearly every weekend from May to August, we piled into our boat and headed up the Taku River to our cabin, about a two-hour trip if we were lucky enough not to get stuck on a sandbar in front of a freezing glacier. The water would go from a blackish-green to the putty color of glacial silt, a signal we were getting closer.

Going to another place was a big deal.

Boundaries were clear.

Florida seemed messy, unplanned. One city slopped into another. We never passed through unsettled territory. Even empty fields were fenced. People, houses, buildings, and roads were everywhere.

I couldn't describe the feeling then, but in retrospect, it shook my sense of place. Lots of people are from sloppy places, where one town grows into another. Other people casually drive through these places, invaders without even knowing it. How unsettling.

By the time we took this family vacation, there already had been four capital move votes — two before I was born. There would later be five more votes. I finally got to cast a ballot myself during the last one, in 1994.

Of the nine ballot questions relating to the capital move since the first one in 1960, only two have been victories for pro-movers. A quick review:

• Aug. 9, 1960: To relocate the capital somewhere "within the Cook Inlet-Railbelt area," the site to be chosen later by a governor-appointed committee, failed 44 percent to 56 percent.

• Nov. 6, 1962: To relocate the capital in "western Alaska, to a site not within thirty miles of Anchorage." A committee of senators would pick three locations, from which voters would have the final say. The state would provide an unknown amount of planning and construction money. This one failed 45 percent to 55 percent.

• Aug. 27, 1974: To construct a new capital city at a site that included "at least 100 square miles of donated and public land, in western Alaska, at least thirty miles from Anchorage and Fairbanks." A governor-appointed committee would nominate two or three sites, with a general election vote determining the final site. The ballot measure again contained no estimated cost, but the "donated and public land" must have sounded good. Voters approved it 56.7 percent to 43.3 percent.

• Nov. 2, 1976: A Capital Site Selection Committee put before voters three choices for the new capital, after spending two years and thousands of dollars: Larsen Lake, Mount Yenlo or Willow. "None of the Above" was not a choice. Willow won the contest with 53.3 percent. Again no price tag was included.

• Nov. 7, 1978: A group from Fairbanks calling itself Frustrated Responsible Alaskans Needing Knowledge — FRANK — launched a drive to require that "all costs of the capital relocation be determined." The costs were to include moving personnel and offices, planning and construction, and furnishings "equal to those at the current capital" and in keeping with the 1974 vote. This reasonable measure, with the heavyweights in Anchorage fighting full bore against it, won 55.7 percent to 44.3 percent.

• Nov. 7, 1978: A separate question estimated the new capital city at $966 million in bonds. It failed overwhelmingly, with only 26.2 percent in favor to 73.8 percent opposed.

• Nov. 2, 1982: Voters trudged to the polls yet again.

This time, the New Capital Site Planning Commission hired a dozen consultants to prepare a twelve-volume report on the move. The state spent $1.8 million on studies. (By comparison, $2.8 million was spent for the first capital planning committees in 1976 and 1978.) Total move costs were pegged at $2.8 billion, which rightfully included $589 million in compensation for losses Juneau residents and businesses would experience with an exodus of two-thirds of the city's population. The measure failed, with 47 percent in favor and 52.8 percent opposed.

• Nov. 8, 1994: Rep. Pat Carney of Wasilla mounted another capital-move effort. This one proposed to simply declare Carney's hometown to be the state's new capital. It failed, with 45.3 percent in favor and 54.6 percent opposed.

• Nov. 8, 1994: Another rendition of the FRANK initiative was approved by 64.2 percent. A stubborn 35.7 percent voted against such disclosure.

Stupid as they may be, capital movers sure are persistent. Over the years they've spent huge sums on ad campaigns (though, arguably, the largest "ads" were free, found on the news and editorial pages of the now-defunct *Anchorage Times*, which campaigned unabashedly in favor of the move) as well as hundreds and hundreds of hours of volunteer time in support of the effort.

I have some theories on why the capital move keeps coming back at us. The main reason is that the rich and powerful of Anchorage, Alaska's largest city with roughly half the state's population, want the convenience of government in their back yard. This makes it easier to lobby legislators and cut deals with governors. They don't care if their cockamamie idea devastates an entire town and surrounding region.

Another reason is the general distrust and disdain for government and elected officials. Attacking Juneau is a quick and dirty cure-all for people with any gripe about state government.

But a third reason the issue won't die is that on its face — and this is hard for me to admit — it sounds somewhat appealing, maybe even reasonable, to move the capital closer to the center of the state's population. Once you get beyond catchy slogans and sound bites, though, you realize that the costs would be prohibitive and that Anchorage would become even more powerful than it already is, to the detriment of every little burg and island outside it.

Like I said earlier, at the time of our Florida vacation, I was only twelve. I wasn't a politically sophisticated pre-teen, and was only dimly aware of the big debate, particularly how access factored into it. I knew the capital could potentially be moved to Willow. I'd seen the "Where in the hell is Willow, Alaska?" bumper stickers. My dad told me Juneau could become a ghost town if the capital moved to Willow, and he'd pound his fist and use expletives like "Bastards!" when he'd talk about it.

From the back seat in Florida, I watched one town blur into another and declared, "I'm glad there are no roads at home. I wouldn't want people from other places driving through it."

"Baby, a road would really be a good thing for Juneau," my dad said. "We really want a road to Juneau. It would be good for the legislature."

I knew where the Capitol was in Juneau. But if I'd ever been in the building at that point, I don't remember it. The

Capitol wasn't part of a single field trip in either elementary, junior high, or high school. And my parents certainly never took me there. (Why would they? It wasn't on the way to the Taku River.) I never saw the legislature in action until I didn't live in Juneau anymore, and was sent to cover it as a reporter for the *Fairbanks Daily News-Miner* in 1993.

After that, I lived in the Capitol during sessions for the next three years. Working until 11 P.M. was standard fare. I haunted the halls, stalked lawmakers with pad and pen poised, and pored over budgets and bills.

My husband, working for a television station at the time, even proposed to me on the floor of the House. Not coincidentally, he asked the late Rep. Ron Larson of Palmer — a former member of the New Capital Site Planning Commission and a staunch pro-mover — to read a citation "honoring the commencement of the lasting joint venture." The citation reads, in part: "Whereas Brian O'Donoghue loves Kate Ripley, a Juneau gal appreciative of sled dogs and possessing every other quality desirable in a wife — even if she does stubbornly oppose the obvious merits of relocating the state capital… "

When I was covering the legislature, I spent so much time working I rarely saw old friends or relatives. I thought nothing was more important than what was happening "on the second floor," as the legislative chambers are referred to, or on "the third floor," where the governor's office is housed. Sometimes I'd be dismayed to pick up a *News-Miner* and find a story I'd written tucked away on an inside page.

Once, late in the session, I stepped outside to grab lunch. It was a sunny day and the air smelled like spruce buds. The summer tour season hadn't started yet, so people on the street were just regular folks, running errands and going about their day. I bumped into an old friend who worked at the police station. She had no idea about an ongoing, dramatic standoff between the Speaker of the House and Senate President.

The contrast between the two worlds was stark, the political buzzing within the Capitol's walls compared to everyday life outside it. The self-important rush of a legislative staffer in the hallway, versus a secretary's rush through Foodland on her lunch hour.

"It doesn't matter where the capital is," I thought to myself. "It may as well be on another planet."

Some day I'll return to my hometown for good, I'm sure of that. My parents, in their sixties and grandparents to our two boys, are the big draw. The Taku River is the other.

For me, "home" and "isolation" go hand in hand. We Ripleys/Niemis/Fleeks/Bergs/Cashels/Ol'gins have always lived in isolated places. Even Douglas Island didn't get its bridge to Juneau until 1935.

I don't doubt another capital move vote, or maybe even several, will come during my lifetime. But these days, efforts to link Juneau to the road system are getting more attention than grand plans for a new capital city.

A road to Juneau would make no difference to the movers. The capital would still be too far away. It would still be the evil seat of state government. It would still be on another planet.

Building a road would accomplish only one thing: It would make my most favorite place in the world a little bit more like everywhere else. ⬧

Sharon Palmisano

Cathy Carpenter Janvrin was born in Louisville, Kentucky, in 1952. Her family moved to Alaska in 1955.

Drawn to the Tundra

Cathy Carpenter Janvrin

It was the smell that got me and still holds me, the piney aroma of Labrador tea.

Nose deep in the miniature forest, sun on my back, the sounds of my friends picking berries nearby grew distant and there was nothing but me and tundra and the sheer gluttonous joy of blueberries, blackberries, and salmonberries to the horizon.

That sunny afternoon more than forty years ago in Bethel isn't a memory so much as it is flashes of consciousness; of the child I once was, of summer days exploring the tundra in glorious freedom, of sweet blueberries warmed by the sun. One whiff of tundra perfumed by Labrador tea brings it all back.

There is no one so free as a happy child in the Bush.

It's those fragile yet enduring moments that, every fall, I try to re-create when the berries are ripe. And why not? Children take joy where they find it; adults have to work at it.

My moments of joy come most plentifully when

picking berries. A natural aromatherapy makes me giddy.

When I first moved to Anchorage from Bethel I didn't know where to begin looking for berries. The city was too big and overwhelming. Discoveries came gradually and mostly by chance; blueberries spotted along the roadside on the way back from an autumn trip to Fairbanks were the first.

The next big break came when hiking around Flattop Mountain one day with my husband and children. A howling mountain wind came out of nowhere and brought on a fierce earache. No one else was ready to leave so I hunkered down in a thicket to wait for the wind to die down. It was blueberry heaven, blueberry magic. The bushes draped my shoulders as I lay back on the soft ground. I filled a plastic bag and my coat pocket and, eventually, my husband's hat. Then we headed down the mountain and home to make two pies for dinner. We never found that particular spot again.

Sometimes, when happily piling provisions into a pack in preparation for a trip, I think of Alaska Native women of not that long ago — and some even today. My berry picking is an indulgence; theirs was survival. Every bit of food they packed was gathered and prepared with their own hands and labor or that of their kin. The thought is humbling. Surely I would starve if I had to depend on my own hard work and skill for my food.

One of my sisters has a friend in the coastal village of Scammon Bay who would qualify for a master's degree in berry picking. The woman's family members pick their own so she has more than she needs. Last fall she gave my sister a five-gallon can of blueberries and a five-gallon can of salmonberries. Now that's a friend. That's generosity.

Personally, I feel mighty big if I'm able to part with a couple of pints for someone who can't get out and about anymore. I'm working on this shameful part of my personality, but for me berry picking — indeed, harvesting of all kinds — contains a significant element of the greedy little kid I was. The child who always wanted the biggest piece of cake, the most cookies, and more Halloween candy grew into an adult who believes it is impossible to have too many berries in the freezer.

Question: What does a berry picker want? Answer: More. At harvest time a stranger's crab apples are in definite danger from me. It's only the fear of getting caught that keeps me away. A friend learned the hard way not to invite me over to pick his currants, which he doesn't want, until he has picked his raspberries, which he does want.

Berry picking is hard labor, if you think of it that way; I do it for love but I'd never do it for money. Ten months of the year I'm naturally as lazy as it is possible to be and still function. I wouldn't walk across the street to ooh and aah over a box filled with diamonds. But when fall comes I haul my middle-aged body up hummocky hillside and treacherous slope in search of ruby low-bush cranberries or sapphire blueberries in hiding amid the foliage.

You can guess a berry picker's age by the sighs and groans she makes after several hours of bending over, squatting down, getting up, stepping over logs, bending over, squatting down, getting up, and so on.

"Let me see if I have this straight," my doctor said the last time I was forced to see him, leaning back in his chair and glaring at my badly swollen knee. "You're overweight and out of shape and you suddenly decide to run up and down a mountain?"

I thought about it.

"Well, yeah," I said. "I was picking berries."

I've picked with equally crazed friends when the ground was so wet that we had to wring out our socks before getting into the car to head for the comforts of a nearby lodge and steaming bowls of soup to stop uncontrollable shivering.

Compatible people are important for good berry-picking forays, the kind of friends who make long road trips bearable because of their humor, their conversation, their zeal for the chase. I've found to my surprise that the friend-ships developed through berry picking are as precious as the berries. I only pick with people I care about or want to know better.

You need to travel with the kind of friends who remain pleasant during a two-night, three-day stay in a rustic National Park Service cabin across from Homer, even though the rain never really stops and the berries we came so far for are covered with worms. You need to travel with friends who remain pleasant even after they discover that everybody brought already peeled snack carrots and no-body brought much in the way of chocolate. If, like me, you don't know much about fending for yourself, you need to travel with friends who are capable, who can put up tents, make fires and brew coffee — and who are willing to take you along. Good friends help you enjoy the beauty that is so close at hand in Alaska.

Some would argue that Anchorage, where I live, isn't really Alaska at all, just close to it. Close to it is good enough for me. Within ten minutes I can be at my favorite wild currant patch or tramping through bushes loaded with high-bush cranberries, raspberries, and rose hips. Twenty minutes takes me to a magnificent blueberry hill with views of the city, the inlet and mountain ranges.

Ordinarily I so loathe car rides that I don't even drive the ten miles to Eagle River. My husband has tried in vain to get me to take a forty-minute ride down to see a friend's nursery full of flowers and fields of tulips. Flowers don't get me out of my chair. But in pursuit of berries, I've headed north hundreds of miles past Paxson and south hundreds of miles past Homer. In the course of those road trips I've been entranced by pods of belugas chasing salmon in Cook Inlet, played with starfish on the beach, sat spellbound at a loon's call. I've marveled at the beauty of rain forest and alpine slope, of quiet inlet at sunset and rushing river in the morning. I've watched a bright sun cut a swath across a mountainside — a mountainside where the berries are, of course.

Wandering through the rain forest around Girdwood one afternoon, I stepped over a fallen log and into smelly, rotting muck that seemed to want to suck my shoes off. It left stains that never came out of my shoes and jeans, but from that muck springs much of the rain forest life. Stains are a fact of life for pickers, and purple fingers and lips are a dead giveaway to your boss that yesterday's bout of stomach flu could better be characterized as berry fever.

As with any outdoor experience, you never know exactly what's going to happen when you head out for berries.

Once, overcome by lust, I hopped from clump to clump of bright red cranberries without noticing where I was going. When my friend and I headed back to the car for a snack we found that the woods looked the same in every direction. The nearby road had disappeared. We tried to find the road by sound, only to discover that what we thought were cars was the wind in the trees or a plane overhead. The wind's song, which had been pleasing background music, now became the eerie overture to a movie with a sad ending. I berated myself for leaving behind food and water and warm clothing, thinking they weren't needed because, after all, we could see the car from where we were.

By luck, we crashed through the trees and discovered the road. We'd been walking parallel to it and could have easily walked for hours without intersecting. We were lost for only twenty minutes or so but my mouth was dry with fear. Neither of us had the heart to go back in that day. We moved on to a lodge and pie and coffee instead, resolving not to make that mistake again.

Picking high-bush salmonberries along a train track one day, I was so mesmerized by the berries' vivid candy colors of yellow, orange, and red that I didn't notice the train barreling around a curve at me. "Jump," my husband yelled, and I did. Before that moment I believed any fool could hear a train coming. Now I know it's far from a sure thing.

Bears are a constant companion in a picker's mind. They like berries too. But what can you do? If you want berries you have to go to bear country. My way of coping, since I don't yet know how to use a gun — and I'm not sure how much good it would do anyway — is with pure, abject fear and superstition. I refuse to say the word "bear" while in their territory. It makes me extremely uncomfortable when other people say it around me, but I try not to inflict my superstitious behavior on them. Again, this is where good friends come in: You want to pick with people you can outrun. Just kidding. You want to pick with people you're happy to chat with, loudly, for hours, so the bears know you're there and will, you hope, seek a quieter spot.

Berry picking is time to revel in the passion of autumn. The finest summer day is bland compared to fall's wanton appeal, when the very air seems to say, "boogie while you can," and the pressure of berries unpicked gets overwhelming as mornings turn chilly.

When berries are ripe, pickers get focused on the harvest and give short shrift to family and work responsibilities. I told my daughter one morning in August that I was going picking but that I planned on being home in time to make a nice dinner, unless the berries were really good. My daughter, who knows me too well, replied, "That doesn't sound promising." And she was right.

Harvesting the fruits of fall, whether berries or apples or potatoes, is a way to cling to the season just passed. A jar of cranberry sauce opened for Thanksgiving dinner, when the deep dark of winter is settling in, brings memories of sun and summer. Blueberry syrup over hot pancakes on a cold morning reminds us that it was warm once and will be again.

Winter is coming and it's time to prepare, by putting up food, by basking in the last of the season's sun, by creating moments of joy that make life worth living. And for some of us, by recreating moments of joy from a childhood that moves farther away with every season.

Fran Durner

Kim Rich, author of the memoir Johnny's Girl, *lives in Anchorage where she is learning to mix martinis and dance the rhumba.*

Tony, a Pink Dress and an Automatic Transmission

Kim M. Rich

I have no nostalgia for my youth. But I seem to have developed a certain nostalgia for my parents' youth. I think it all started with the new car.

Last year, at age 41, I bought my first, what I call *real*, adult car. A mid-size, luxury sedan that I fell in love with the moment I opened the door and gazed upon its calm-inducing yards of beige, buttery, all-leather interior. But before anyone can understand the significance of this car, I need to talk about the others — my *ex*-cars.

My first was a VW bug I bought in 1978. Model year? I can't remember. It was old. I thought it was cute. I was nineteen when I bought it for a few hundred dollars. It was dark green. What I remember best about this car was the broken windshield wipers. I had to yank a string to pull them back and forth.

It's important to note that I lived in Juneau with this car, where it rains an average of fifty-four inches a year. I was young, what can I say? Stupid too, I guess. This car handled poorly in icy conditions. It tended to slide backward, sideways, and into ditches. The car also featured a hole in the back floorboard that was covered with a piece of plywood. I didn't even know it was there until a friend accidentally dislodged it one night when I was driving down North Douglas Highway, going about forty-five miles per hour (the VW's top speed). My companion's foot fell through the floor, and for a brief moment I looked like I was in Bedrock, driving the Flintstone's mobile. This promptly woke my friend from his drunken stupor.

My second car was a used, ugly brown, Datsun B-210. This was before I had any money to speak of, and before I had any taste. It's hardly worth mentioning. I soon dumped the Datsun and bought a nifty 1980 Toyota Tercel, also used, but in like-new condition.

Now, that car I liked. Not loved, mind you, but liked. It was a handsome little silver coupe, featuring an AM/FM radio, and a black, all vinyl interior which I scrupulously polished to a brilliant sheen once a week with Armor All. I should have owned stock in Armor All.

I moved up fairly quickly after that. Next came the red, Mazda 323 sedan. *Cloth* interior, AM/FM radio, and *cassette* stereo, and which I bought brand, spanking new right off the lot in what was probably one of the most exciting periods of my life. I had just turned 30 that year; the same year I got a big fancy literary agent, sold the film rights to my life story, AND the book rights to pen my memoir. (Note, I did not buy a BMW, a Mercedes, or a Porsche. Go back to the beginning and read the part about having a *literary* agent. Not a sports agent. Not a movie actor's agent. That's literary agent. That means I'm a writer. That means I buy a Mazda 323.)

I had nowhere to go but up from there. So what came next? No car at all. I traded in the Mazda for public transportation three years later when I moved to New York City to attend graduate school.

As you can see, most of my life I bought practical, modestly priced, all imported/all-boring cars. My latest car, while not exactly flashy, is American-made and cost double what the Mazda did. Nonetheless, it is a *reasonably* priced luxury sedan.

When I owned the Mazda, my hipper friends wondered about my overall hipness. "What's with the sedan?" one coupe-driving, swingin' single, male pal asked, as if I'd just bought a Ford Country Squire station wagon with the fake wood-paneled siding. But now, at my age, no one wonders any longer about my choice of vehicles. Mine is a car for mid-life.

I am, nonetheless, still out of step in a place where car owners favor big macho trucks (my husband), big macho sport utility vehicles (most everyone else), and unmacho mini-vans. My new car's standard equipment and options? Mid-sized, V-6, sunroof, heated front passenger seats, AM/FM, cassette *and* CD player, automatic transmission (my first), dark red exterior paint. *Beautiful.* This is the first car I have ever loved. Maybe not passionately, say, like I might love a '67 Corvette Stingray or a '65 Mustang. But I love it enough. It's, as they say, a nice ride.

No sooner had I bought the car, than I got the Tony Bennett CD, as if getting behind the wheel of my new car required it.

I have long been a fan of pop singers and crooners. Frank Sinatra, Dean Martin, Sammy Davis Jr., and the like. This music resonates with me because it was the music my parents loved. These recording artists were probably the first I heard, while lying in my crib.

There were lots of others. I learned to twist to Chubby Checker. Gag if you will, but I like the Elvis of the late 1960s and early 1970s; I actually dig "Burning Love" and "Suspicious Minds." My father ran a night club for a while and I still remember being entranced when someone would punch up Percy Sledge's "When a Man Loves a Woman" on the jukebox. I was ten years old and I was riveted.

The other day, my husband and I attended a dance concert and the dancers performed to a song that I had not heard since I was a kid. Later, my husband commented aloud how much he liked the song and wondered what the title was and who performed it. The answer just sprang from my mouth: "River Deep, Mountain High," Ike and Tina Turner.

My father had reel-to-reel stereo player/recorders long before anybody else. He had an eight-track tape player in his car as soon as they hit the market. I used to ride around with him when he'd make his rounds at night, from bar to bar, collecting debts or rounding up gamblers for a game of poker.

I'd sit in the car while he went into the strip clubs — The Sand Box or The Embers or Club China Doll. I'd listen to whatever he owned at the time — Neil Diamond "Live at the Greek" theater in Berkeley or Johnny Rivers at Hollywood's Whiskey A Go-Go. For me, cars are about music, and vice versa. That was the one thing I missed when riding the subways and buses in New York

City; no music, unless I lugged along a Walkman, or some kid from the Bronx boarded with his boom box.

For a while in the early 1970s, my father subscribed to Billboard magazine. And for a while, Billboard used to include posters from the album covers of hot new acts. In seventh grade, my musical tastes ran more toward the milquetoast sound of the Carpenters or the band, Bread. (Forgive me. Later it was Black Sabbath; God knows why. Much later, Led Zeppelin, because that's what everyone else listened to. Later came Crosby, Stills, Nash & Young, Carole King, and Elton John.) But before I developed my own taste in music, I had Joe Cocker, "Mad Dogs and Englishmen," and Quicksilver Messenger Service posters on my wall. I didn't even listen to these bands, but I knew who they were.

This was before my friends and I would find ourselves immersed in our own version of the counterculture — hiking boots, long skirts, and down coats, worn like a uniform, to go along with our misguided dreams of moving to California, or Homer, to live in a commune.

All this was thanks to something known as the "back to nature" movement. We were living surrounded by more nature than anyone could possibly want and yet we felt compelled to live in even more of it. For a brief period of my misspent youth, I aspired to live a rural lifestyle. One with no running water, no electricity, and all wood heat. Like people in India. Now you're beginning to see why I have no nostalgia for my youth. It was *no* fun.

Because of my father's influence, I went to concerts when most of the kids my age were still going to Scout meetings. I saw Jefferson Airplane at age twelve. Fats

Domino, too, because my dad promoted the show. I saw the movie "Woodstock" when it came out, *accompanied by my father*. I saw "Alice's Restaurant" when I was in sixth grade.

Fact is, I like all music, just like my father, who had eclectic taste in popular music — pop, rock, blues, jazz. You name it. Maybe the only thing he didn't listen to much was country, very little folk, and certainly no bluegrass. But then again Patsy Cline was in the house. The Kingston Trio, too.

I still like it all. But these days, when I'm in The Car, I listen to Tony and Frank and I am transported; not only to my destination, but also in time. I am no longer in my own car, in the year 2000. I am somewhere in the early to mid-1960s. I am in my father's Cadillac, the white one, the convertible. Or so I am told because I don't actually remember his first Cadillac. I do remember his second one, the Bronzit Eldorado he drove in the early 1970s. I have no nostalgia for that car. I rode in it when I was a teenager, when I was trying to get "back to nature." Our rides together were rarely happy occasions then. Few teen-parent get-togethers are.

Sometime between the white Cadillac and the Eldorado was a forest green Monte Carlo. A coupe, as I recall, but a step up size-wise, with better passenger capacity than his previous car, an El Camino. Not a bad car either. Like music, my father loved cars. Used to sell them when he was a teenager and when he first moved to Anchorage in 1958. If he were around now, we could talk about both. I'd like that. But he's been gone a long time. More than half my life.

Within the same year that I bought The Car, I bought an expensive cocktail dress. They call them that now, too. But this dress was not designed with my generation in mind. Pink, with sequins and lace, it seems designed for my generation's fond remembrance of the generation that came before. Of a more formal time, of cocktail parties and *real* cocktails served in smoke-filled rooms, where LPs were slipped onto the hi-fi phonograph encased in the sturdy walnut cabinet.

Like the car, the dress was bought using some subconscious impulse. I got it home and dug out a family photo album and found it to be nearly identical to a white cocktail dress my mother wore on Christmas, 1963.

When I wear the dress, I am in my parent's living room; in the small white house on Fireweed Lane. I am listening to their recording of "Camelot" from the Broadway show. Or I am in the middle of one of their many parties. The living room is filled with men in suits and women in cocktail dresses, all laughing and talking, all on their way out or just in from an evening at the Pink Poodle Lounge.

When I drive in my new luxury car, I feel my father's presence. I feel an overwhelming sense of longing for a place, a time, and two people no longer here. Both of my parents died young; both before they got to the age I am now. Both were dead before their middle years, when they, in turn, could buy a mid-life crisis car.

So I am left to remember for them. *Their* youth. My childhood. The earliest part, when I first fell in love, with music, with them, and Tony Bennett. 🍃

Kathy Doogan

Mike Doogan was born in Fairbanks and lives in Anchorage, where he writes a column for the Anchorage Daily News.

Muscle Memory

Mike Doogan

I awoke with a jerk from a dream of falling. My watch said 5:30. Richard rolled out of his sleeping bag and into his clothes. He unzipped the doorway and hoisted himself out of the tent with a groan. I followed. The world looked gray and flat and ghostly. The forest smelled wet and rank. A squirrel scolded the morning from a nearby spruce: *chit-chit-chit-chitchitchitchit*. Metal clinked on metal and voices murmured. I twisted and turned and stretched to loosen up my muscles.

We were at Sheep Camp on the Chilkoot Trail. During the winter of 1897-98, Sheep Camp was a sprawling collection of white duck tents surrounded by snow-covered piles of boxes and bags, men coming and going, stovepipes sending wood smoke to the noses of small, wild animals who watched all this activity with fear and wonder. In the summer of 1998, Sheep Camp was a couple of dozen tent sites, two warm-up shacks, two outhouses and two, tall inverted U's of pipe to hang food out of the reach of bears. Then and now, Sheep Camp was the last camp before the summit of Chilkoot Pass.

Richard returned from the bear bag pole with our food. He took the one-burner stove out of the bag, set it on a stump and lit a match. The stove whooshed to life. I broke camp while he cooked. Breakfast was a thermal mug of coffee and a plastic bowl of oatmeal and brown sugar. The mixture was hot and sweet. Warmth rolled to the tips of my fingers and toes. People carrying packs passed by in groups of two or three, misshapen, other-wordly figures in the dim light.

"See you at the summit!" they called. "Klondike or bust!"

I carried the dishes to the river. The river was wide and shallow, a sparkling sheet rushing over stones. The water numbed my hands. Richard came and began pumping water into plastic bottles. We finished breaking camp, stuffing everything into our packs. We took a last look around our campsite, then hoisted our packs onto our backs. In Skagway mine had weighed fifty pounds. With his camera gear, Richard's had weighed sixty. I settled the pack straps onto my shoulders, cinched up the waist belt.

"Yukon, ho," Richard said and set off up the trail. I followed.

The Chilkoot Trail is thirty-three miles long. It climbs from the Alaska coast through Chilkoot Pass in the Coast Mountains to the headwater lakes of the Yukon River. One hundred years before, from the fall of 1897 to the spring of 1898, thousands of people had struggled along this trail, bound for the Klondike gold fields. They were people of every sort. I have read accounts of the stampede written by an Irish peasant and a Minnesota pharmacist and a Chicago housewife. But the stampeders were mainly middle-aged, middle-class American men who knew next to nothing about the north, mining or the outdoors.

We have a hard time understanding the Klondike Gold Rush today. In the age of the jet airplane, it is hard to imagine how far away the Klondike was. In the age of the computer, it is hard to imagine how little information was available. We have no real comprehension of how important gold was to the American economy of the time, or of the restless spirit of men whose fathers had fought the Civil War. Historians estimate that about one hundred thousand people started for the Klondike that fall, and that about half of them made it the next spring. Imagine one hundred thousand otherwise ordinary people, with no special knowledge or training, setting off for Antarctica to mine silicon for computer chips.

What seems like an aberration in the history of the United States was a watershed event in the history of the north. The fifty thousand people who reached the Klondike quintupled the population of northern North America. Before the gold rush, most of the people who lived in Alaska and the Yukon were Natives. Forever after, most were white.

Richard and I walked steadily uphill for the first hour. He had decided to walk in shorts and a T-shirt and I copied him. I was cold at first, but the walking soon warmed me. As the day grew brighter, birds began to rustle and sing. We were still in the forest, but it was not the forest we had started out in. Down on the coast, the trail was walled by thick, leafy stands of alder and willow and head-high devil's club, roofed by the branches of giant

Sitka spruce, western hemlock, and black cottonwood. Walking along it had been like walking along a moist, fragrant, green tunnel. Here, higher, the soil was spread thinner over the bedrock. The trees and bushes were shorter and did not stand so close together. More of the water that fell from the sky rushed downhill. In the first half hour, we crossed seven bridges, clomped along five sections of boardwalk, splashed through two creeks. Over the tops of the dwindling trees I could see the sheer, gray-black walls of the narrowing canyon. Here and there the rock face had been scoured by avalanches.

This was our third day on the trail. The soles of my feet hurt from walking on rocks and roots. My leg muscles hurt from climbing up and down. My back muscles ached from sleeping on the ground. My shoulder muscles ached from the pack. My skin and scalp itched from not bathing. My arms and legs itched from bug bites. I wondered why none of the many literary works I'd read about nature ever mentioned the discomforts. How could anyone love nature with a face full of no-see-'ums?

I don't love nature. When I was growing up in the sparsely settled interior of Alaska, we were concerned with protecting ourselves against nature and using it for our benefit. No one I knew went into the woods for any but the most practical reasons. Even my Boy Scout forays were more practical than recreational: winning woodcraft merit badges, passing cold weather tests, cutting wood for sale. In this attitude, at least, I am not all that much different from the stampeders. For them, nature was something to use or pass through as quickly as possible.

Few of the stampeders knew the best way to get to the

gold fields. Some took the rich man's route: by boat from Seattle to Saint Michael at the mouth of the Yukon, then upriver by shallow-draft steamboat. But most couldn't afford the fares and freight charges. So they tried other routes: overland from Edmonton, across the glaciers above Valdez, up the Stikine River. The majority took boats from Seattle to the sudden towns of Skagway and Dyea. They swarmed over the White Pass Trail from Skagway to Lake Bennett; over this trail, the Chilkoot, from Dyea to Lake Lindemann.

The challenge was more than just getting themselves to the Klondike. When the Canadians realized a multitude was going to converge on a piece of their wilderness, the government issued an order that every stampeder had to bring along enough food and gear for one year. This amounted to about a ton of goods. The North West Mounted Police enforced the order; at the top of Chilkoot Pass they set up a machine gun just in case the crowd got out of hand. They didn't need it. The stampeders were law-abiding folks, and they obeyed the order.

A typical stampeder brought along 400 pounds of flour, 150 pounds of bacon, 150 pounds of peas, 100 pounds of beans, 100 pounds of sugar, 75 pounds of dried fruit, 40 of rolled oats, 25 pounds of rice, 25 pounds of dried potatoes, 25 pounds of butter, 15 pounds of coffee, 10 pounds of tea, 10 pounds of salt, 8 pounds of baking powder, a pound of pepper, a gallon of vinegar, 1 1/2 pounds of beef extract, four packages of yeast cakes, and eighteen cans of condensed milk. He also carried a frying pan, plates, a tin cup, a coffee pot, knives, forks and spoons, a cooking pan, a whipsaw, a handsaw, a jack plane, an ax, a hatchet, a shovel, a pick, a drift pick, a whetstone, an emery stone, files, a brace and bits, chisels, a drawknife, a single block, a solder outfit, tool handles, nails, oakum, pitch, rope, a two-foot rule, a medicine chest, a gold pan, a wash basin, a tent, a sleeping bag, towels, candle wick, a miner's candlestick, a compass, pack straps, granite buckets, and a Yukon stove. Plus clothing and whatever personal possessions he thought advisable.

Moving all this material was not easy. The Chilkoot and White Pass trails were popular because, as rugged as they were, once a stampeder got his goods to the lakes and built his boat, he could count on the Yukon River to carry him and his belongings to the Klondike. Many stampeders carried every pound of their outfits with their own muscles. This made for slow going. The preferred method was to shuttle the goods from spot to spot. Shuttling his ton five miles, fifty or sixty pounds a trip, could take a stampeder a month. He had no way to guard his goods at either end of the shuttle, but he didn't really need one. The honesty of the stampeders extended to the goods of others; there were few thefts.

Some stampeders formed syndicates for the adventure and worked in groups to reach the Klondike. Commercial help was available, too, for those who could afford it. On both the Chilkoot and White Pass trails, people packed for pay. The Chilkoot was too steep for horses, but on the White Pass, pack trains carried goods. Enterprising businessmen built tramways on the Chilkoot to lift freight to the summit. Towns sprang up at intervals that matched the shuttle distances, offering hot meals and hot baths and gear of all sorts. The towns dried up, but their names live on. The first day we walked eight miles, past Finnegan's Point to Canyon City. The second day we walked five miles, past Pleasant Camp to Sheep Camp.

We were walking now on Long Hill, a three-mile stretch of trail that rises 1,700 feet before reaching The Scales. Some sections of the trail were so steep that they were like short flights of stairs. We walked single file and didn't talk much. At the end of the first hour we were still in the forest, although the trees were short and the ground cover was as much moss as plants. We could not find a flat spot to stop. We climbed off the trail, leaned back against rocks and shrugged off our packs. I flexed my shoulder muscles. The light wind found where I had sweated through my T-shirt under the pack and cooled me. I dug gorp and peanut butter Power Bars out of my pack. We ate and drank water for a while. We had had overcast the first day, rain the second. But the clouds were trailing away overhead, leaving behind more and more blue. High above, a speck of a jet drew a narrow, arrow-straight vapor trail across the sky.

"We couldn't ask for a finer day," Richard said. He was smiling, his teeth showing white through his salt and pepper beard. Richard and I have been friends for fifteen years. He runs the photo department at the newspaper where I work. We were, both of us, forty-nine, born within ten days of one another, but Richard seemed to grow younger with each day on the trail. "In the woods," Emerson wrote, "a man casts off his years, as the snake his slough, and at what period soever of life, is always a child. In the woods, is perpetual youth." Like Emerson, Richard had been born in Massachusetts. His love for the wild had pulled him west, then north, to hike, climb mountains, guide and take photographs. I had been telling him gold rush stories for a couple of years. His response was to want to walk the ground. Like Thoreau, he believed that "an absolutely new prospect is a great happiness."

Richard and I got into our packs again and started walking. I warmed up quickly in the sunshine. We followed the trail up and around a sharp corner and were suddenly out of the forest. The Taiya River, which we had been following since the trailhead, was now nothing more than a series of waterfalls that plunged down the rock faces of the canyon, then spurted downhill in a dozen freshets. We were surrounded by rock: rock walls and rocky ground, some of it barren, some mossy. Wherever the rocks had collected enough dirt, isolated thickets of willow and alder grew. Small stands of dwarf spruce sprouted in sheltered places. Higher up I could see patches of snow. The trail ended at the base of a long, sloping jumble of jagged rock, the residue of dozens of avalanches.

"This might be tricky," Richard said. His years in the outdoors made him the expert of our team, so I paid attention to what he told me. "Make sure the rock you're stepping onto can take your weight. Don't start hopping."

He began climbing over the rocks. I tried to follow in his footsteps, but he soon pulled ahead. I was left to pick my own way up the rock fall. Rocks shifted as I stepped on them and I teetered. I moved more slowly. My pack rocked back and forth as I walked, threatening to throw me off balance. I moved even more slowly. The universe shrank to the next rock and the next and the next. The rock fall was a couple of hundred yards long and it took me a couple of hundred years to cross it. Richard was waiting on the far side. I took off the broad-brimmed felt hat I was wearing and wiped my forehead with a bandanna, waiting for my leg muscles to stop trembling.

"That was fun," I said. "Let's go back and do it again."

Most of the stampeders didn't have to worry about these rocks. The timing of the gold rush was this: News of the gold strike arrived in Seattle and San Francisco, in the form of the first Klondike millionaires, in July 1897. The news spread by telegraph and newspaper. But only the quick and resourceful got to the Klondike before the Yukon froze. Most stampeders took a while — a few days, a few weeks — to decide to go. Once they decided, they had to get to a port, buy their outfits, and reach the Alaska coast. By then, winter had come to the Coast Mountains. So for most stampeders the Chilkoot was a trail through the snow. When they reached the still-frozen lakes, they built boats and waited for spring.

Richard set off and I followed. His pack bobbed up and down in front of me, a mass of mends and patches, its once-orange nylon now brown with dirt and age. The plastic water bottle peering from a side pocket was opaque with scratches. My own pack was bright blue. My polypropylene T-shirt and nylon hiking shorts had never been dirty before. The trail grew steeper, and I leaned forward more against the weight of my pack, fiddling with the straps from time to time, trying to discover some small comfort. I thought about the stampeders with their own loads. No form-fitting, internal-frame packs for them. At best, straight, hard packboards. At worst, boxes or bags tied to their backs with cat's cradles of rope.

We crossed stretches of dirt and rock and wound past alder thickets and came to the base of another rock fall, this one three or four times as steep and eight or nine times as long. Other hikers were brightly colored, thumb-sized shapes crawling up the slope. The route, marked by orange, metal poles, was along the right side of the rock fall. We started climbing.

We took our second break about halfway up the rock fall. I removed my hat to let my hair dry in the sun. Sweat ran down the back of my neck. I sat and stretched my legs out in front of me. We drank water and ate maple Power Bars.

"The peanut butter ones are better," I said. "If better is a word that has any meaning in this context."

After I finished eating I looked at the map and hiker's guide put out by the National Park Service. We had some walking ahead of us. "Do not underestimate the trail or overestimate your abilities," the guide said. "Even if you are lucky enough to have good weather the trail is long and strenuous."

The trail lies in two national parks, one American and the other Canadian, with the border at the summit of the pass. Traffic along it is controlled by permit. No more than fifty people are allowed to cross the summit on a given day. There is a bookletful of other rules. Hikers are required to stay on the marked trail and camp only at official campsites. They are ordered to pack out their garbage and forbidden from picking up any artifacts they might see. They cannot build campfires. The trail has even been relocated in several places, to allow the ground to recover from so many feet and to avoid property now owned by Tlingit or Athabascan Indians. All of this is in sharp contrast to the laissez faire of the stampede. If a stampeder had managed to survive the intervening century, he would have seen few similarities between what we were doing and what he had done.

We shoved things back into our packs and hoisted them onto our backs. Looking up, Richard said, "You can see why that ranger last night called this a route and not a trail. We're climbing now."

We climbed steadily. A few hundred yards of dirt separated the top of the rock fall from a field of snow. The orange trail markers stood out clearly against the white.

"Take big steps on and off," Richard said. "You're most likely to break through at the edges, where the snow is softest."

We slipped and slid up the snowfield, then up bare trail, then up a second snowfield, then up more trail that wound through big, moss-and-lichen-covered domes of cap rock. Just about the time we were due for our third hourly break, we reached The Scales.

The Scales is a sort of bowl at the foot of the steepest part of Chilkoot Pass. Here, one hundred years ago, packers had re-weighed their loads and increased their fees for the struggle up to the summit. The sun was high in the sky and hot. Richard was taking pictures, so I went to stand in the shade of a big rock. A young man was sitting there, his back to the rock. The rock walls now looked close enough to touch. Up ahead and to the left, a tall, steep slope of jagged rocks reached out of sight. The slope led to the summit of the pass. When, in winter, the stampeders reached here, they scaled the slope in steps cut into the snow. They named the slope the Golden Stairs.

"Pretty impressive, isn't it?" I said to the young man.

"Now, we've got something much like this at home," he said in a rolling Irish accent. "Only taller. We call it the devil's tail."

Many of the stampeders were more impressed than the Irishman. They looked at what was ahead of them and quit right here. They sold what they could, left the rest and walked back the way they had come. All around us were the rusting remains of their abandoned teapots and plates and cans, and bits and pieces of the tramways that once, for a fee, carried goods to the summit.

I walked back out into the sunshine and over to where the park service had put up informational markers complete with photographs from the stampede. In one, an Indian woman dressed in dark wool crouched with a group of packers. Roped to her back was a cast iron stove. She looked directly at the camera with eyes as expressionless as black pebbles. I wondered what she must have thought of the stampede, of having all these white men with their strange ways rolling over her country like a flood.

I know a little of being overwhelmed by immigrants myself. The culture of the stampeders who stayed was a prospecting and mining culture, an odd mix of individualism and group responsibility. It survived for many years. Forty-four of the fifty-five people who wrote the Alaska state constitution in 1955-56 were or had been miners, my father among them. I grew up in that culture and lived in it until a flood of oil patch immigrants washed it away in the 1980s.

I had seen plenty of photographs of the gold rush and its era. The camera was the personal computer of its day, newly mobile and affordable. Floyd Winter and Percy Pond, E.A. Hegg and the Kinsey brothers, Clarke and Clarence, are the best known of dozens of photographers who recorded the gold rush and the people who went on it. In each of those photographs, every person has the same dark, unreadable eyes. Every person including the short man in tall boots standing at the head of a train of pack horses in the muddy confusion of a marshaling yard outside Skagway. The man was named John Egbert Feero, and he was my great-grandfather.

When the rush began, Feero was an unemployed, thirty-nine-year-old teamster. He had moved his wife, Emma, and their children to the Washington Territory from Maine in 1888. He opened a freight business in Tacoma, the Puget Sound Transfer Company, and prospered. Another child, Frank, my mother's father, was born a year later. The transfer company went bust during the long, painful, nationwide recession of the 1890s and John Feero did what he could to make ends meet. When he heard of the Klondike gold strike, he saw a chance and took it, borrowing the money for his passage and arriving in Skagway in August 1897.

"He took a horse and a cloth and a pack saddle," his oldest boy, Willie, wrote to an uncle back East the next month. "When he got there he sold his horse for $175 and the pack saddle for $6 and then hired out to the same man for $5 a day and his board and lodging. He has made one trip over the trail, that is, with a pack train. He says the trail is offull bad."

The White Pass Trail was longer than the Chilkoot, but not as steep. That made men think that pack horses were the way to move their tons of goods. But horses were poorly adapted for the rugged, rock-and-root strewn trail. Their handlers were in a hurry, and they took out their frustrations on the horses, overloading them, beating them and not feeding them or caring for them properly. They killed so many horses on the "offull" trail that locals called it the Dead Horse Trail.

"Of all the routes to the Klondike," wrote historian Pierre Berton, "the Skagway trail across the White Pass, more than any other, brought out the worst in men."

But not in John Feero. When, on his first trip with a pack train, he saw how the horses were being treated, he turned around and walked back to Skagway.

"Feero refused to go out on the trail again unless there was proper food for the horses and a wrangler to take care of them en route," wrote Skagway historian Howard Clifford.

Horses were scarce and expensive, and caring for them paid off. Feero was able to send for his family in the fall of 1897. By December his oldest son, Willie, was writing that "Papa has got a pack train of sixteen horses and is doing well here" and "Papa says he's not going to leave hear (sic) until he gets a barrel of money."

John Feero didn't get his barrel of money. He died on the White Pass Trail before 1898 ended. The account of his death I have came in a letter from a friend to Emma Feero's mother in Auburn, Maine. John Feero had gone to Bennett on business and was on his way back, on December 6, 1898, traveling on horseback with a Mr.

Aimery. They ate dinner at Little Meadows, then started for Skagway. Near the summit, a snowstorm hit. They pushed on but lost the trail. They kept going, with Feero complaining of severe stomach pain. About 2 A.M., Aimery reached a railroad construction camp, but when would-be rescuers found Feero lying in the snow he was sleeping "the sleep that knows no awaking in this world."

I had many facts about John Feero, in large part because a distant relation wrote a family history. But I had no sense of the man. In the photos I've seen, he was a small man with a prominent forehead and puffy mustache. I wanted to see something of him in myself, but couldn't. I would have liked to have walked the trail John Feero traveled, but most of it now lies beneath the tracks of the White Pass and Yukon Route Railway.

Richard and I left The Scales and scrambled uphill to the base of the Golden Stairs. The jumble of rock rose more than one thousand feet, much of it at a forty-five-degree angle. When I looked up, my pack tipped my hat over my eyes.

"Well," Richard said, "it's not going to get any shorter standing here."

He started up. I followed. Each time I stopped to catch my breath, Richard was farther above me. Each time I looked up, my pack tried to knock my hat off. When I loosened the straps, the pack swayed dangerously. Halfway up, my calf and thigh muscles began screaming. Sweat ran into my eyes. I nicked a knee on a rock, then a shin. The slope seemed steeper than forty five degrees. Each time I looked down, it seemed I would fall straight to the bottom if I let go. I began to wonder if I would make it. This was,

I realized, as close to the Klondike stampeders as I would get. Tired and uncertain, in the midst of a difficult climb, with a lot of trail left in front of me, I thought I might be able to feel how they had felt. If I just let myself feel the sun on my face and the sweat running down it, listened to the rise and fall of my breathing, felt the nicks on my legs and the tightness of my muscles, I could imagine myself in the gold rush.

But of course I couldn't do that. Instead, I heard the voice of the park ranger from his pre-climb chat of the night before: "Remember, folks, as you climb the Golden Stairs, it took the average stampeder forty trips to get his ton of goods over the top."

I finished the climb and, a few days later, the hike. We rode a steam train back along the White Pass Trail to Skagway. Near the top of the pass, in a light fog, we chugged past a sign that read "Little Meadows." When we reached Skagway, Richard and I checked into the Golden North Hotel, which dates from the gold rush. The rooms at the Golden North are named for Skagway pioneers. On the door of the room I had requested was a brass plate that read, "John and Emma Feero." We took turns bathing in the claw-footed bathtub, then walked to a little restaurant for a big meal. Many of the buildings we passed were replicas of the gold rush era, wooden storefronts with old-timey lettering in their windows: a pharmacy, a saloon, a bank.

When our first cold beer arrived, Richard tilted his bottle toward me.

"To the stampeders," he said. "They must have been tough customers."

We ate big steaks and gooey desserts and walked back to the hotel. Lying in bed, I thought about the week on the trail. I had walked in the footsteps of the gold rush, or as close to them as various park officials would allow. But I didn't seem to feel any closer to the event, or to my own roots in Alaska. I could read about my past and think about it and walk through it, but I couldn't quite touch it. My muscles might feel like they remembered, but my mind refused to believe them. Or so I thought. When I fell asleep, I dreamed I was on a horse in a snowstorm when, suddenly, I was falling.

Paul Estabrook, Mediavine Productions

Howard Weaver was born in Anchorage in 1950 and worked as a newspaperman in Alaska for more than 25 years.

Next Chapter

Howard Weaver

In the past couple of years, I've learned to do a relaxation exercise that involves imagining the most special place I've ever been. I knew without reflection which to choose: a spot beside a driftwood fire on the beach at Aurora Lagoon on Kachemak Bay. In memory the time is late on a summer evening, sunlight slanting in from an improbable angle, falling without warmth but leaving buttery light on the stalks of grass that grow up through the sand.

It's a specific recollection, selected from a deep catalog of days and nights on the bay. I don't expect to find a more beautiful spot in this life, or spend a more contented evening than that night in magical memory. But I haven't been back for more than five years now.

I left Alaska against all expectations — my own and those of nearly everybody else who knew me. Anchorage born, Muldoon reared, Alaska seasoned, I was a lifer if ever there was one. I had a great answer for folks who asked if I'd lived in Alaska all my life: "Not yet," I always replied.

But I can't use that line any more. I rolled into Sacramento, California, on Halloween in 1995 and haven't spent a whole week back in Alaska since. Two quick personal visits — a sick friend, and a brother graduating from the University of Alaska Anchorage — and a short business trip have been all the Alaska I've needed. I expect that to change, but honest appraisal forces me to admit that it hasn't, yet.

I guess I'd been gone a couple of years before I realized I had left Alaska because it broke my heart. Some people get tired of winter; I got tired of the cold-hearted attitudes that were taking over the place I loved so well.

At the time I thought I left for opportunity. After more than twenty year at the *Anchorage Daily News*, battling the *Anchorage Times*, they finally quit. I knew there was still a lot of valuable newspaper work to do in Alaska, but I was forty-five years old and the feeling of finishing up a chapter and turning the page was powerfully upon me. The corporate job exploring Internet publishing in California felt like a damned good chance to start writing a new one.

A couple of years into my new narrative, a friend asked me to write a preface for his book of Alaska oil history. I wrote a thousand words about the state's relationship with Big Oil and showed them to my wife, Barbara. She read it through quietly and said, "You know, this is awfully bitter." I toned it down considerably — I've learned over the years to trust her solid advice — and sent the piece on to the publisher.

"You know," he told me a few weeks later, "this is awfully bitter." I toned it down again, and still ended up with a piece that sometimes occasions comment.

I didn't realize how I felt until I wrote that. I can't find my original draft — Awfully Bitter Number One — but I remember the overwhelming emotion was of loss and mourning. Somewhere between Swanson River and Bligh Reef, the pioneers who settled Alaska became colonists. The homesteaders became company men, the prospect of a paycheck and a Permanent Fund dividend replacing the self sufficiency and community spirit that knitted together earlier generations through so many long, dark winters. Though there was a brief rebellion after the *Exxon Valdez* oil spill, a few months later Alaska's body politic rolled over again and renewed its bargain with the industry: Take what you want; leave money.

I don't blame the big oil companies for acting like big oil companies; they sometimes make me mad, but I expect no better of them. My aching disappointment came from watching Alaska's character change so profoundly.

Over decades in the writing game in Alaska, I suppose I encountered every one of the 6,743 cliches available to describe the place, and none was truer than this: The real Alaska isn't so much a state as a state of mind. Therein lies my problem; while the landscape and the scenery have survived reasonably well over the past thirty years, the collective "state of mind" has deteriorated faster than a spawned-out humpy in fresh water.

Alaskans who used to be routinely generous and optimistic have become selfish. Oh, not everybody, of course not; and not *you*, gentle reader. But far too many of your neighbors.

In a society with no income tax, no sales tax and a two

thousand dollar payment from the state for every man, woman and child, they pushed a tax cap. Public services and public facilities inexorably starve to death; bright new landmarks like the Alaska Center for the Performing Arts already look worn around the edges, and public dollars to fund assistance for the less fortunate have been unapologetically eroded, as well.

The growing selfishness is particularly virulent when it comes to relations between the new majority culture and Alaska Natives — never more evident than in the endless, ugly debates over subsistence hunting and fishing. Yeah, sure, some guy in a Wasilla four-plex has just as much claim on the fish and game as a family on a road-less stretch of the Yukon whose culture has revolved around hunting for 5,000 years. Think Native suicides and alcoholism might be connected to missionaries and the cash economy? "Hey, *I* never did anything to 'em," he might reply.

Alaskans' unwillingness to recognize the unique needs and rights of Native people amount to the continuing rejection of a rare opportunity to blend dominant and indigenous cultures in ways that could have strengthened both. Instead, unconditional surrender is demanded, engulfment *uber alles*.

Hand-in-hand comes the steady deterioration of the authentic in Alaska. Yes, February is still dark and some-times chilly, but there's often little else to distinguish Anchorage from Akron, strip mall alongside franchise next to themed restaurant. Far too little of Alaska's art or music springs from northern soil; it is far more likely to be derivative, a country-cousin copy of something being done Outside. The tourist trade is most often an entirely packaged experience these days, industrial recreation delivered aboard self-contained floating cities.

Alaska is no worse than many places in such matters — but I never expected much of the other places. Alaska was supposed to be special; my affection flagged as I discovered the many ways in which it is not. California's legislature can be as cynical and venal as Alaska's (though seldom as boneheaded), but it doesn't pain me nearly so much to watch them screw up here. I like my new life here and living in California just fine, thank you — but I truly love Alaska.

As a journalist, I still sometimes miss the security of working in my hometown, of knowing the political landscape as intimately as the natural scenery, of feeling sure-footed while navigating the community. About seven months after leaving, a friend wrote with lots of detailed, inside news about the Alaska legislature. Reading his letter and understanding all the nuances, I realized, with some sadness, that I would never again in this life understand anything as fundamentally as I had understood Alaska. The realization came with a distinctly bittersweet twinge.

But I knew that wasn't all bad, either. Being so fluently aware of Alaska was part of what fueled the imperative to leave — to learn something new, to live something different. As Shakespeare said "Things won are done; soul's joy lies in the doing."

And so I left.

I write about this now with some reluctance, for I

know that leaving Alaska feels like betrayal to the folks who stay behind. I know that because I felt it so often myself over those many years. (If you doubt that observation, turn it around and look from the other side: Ever feel anything more satisfying than talking with somebody who left and then moved back, full of stories about how bad things are Out There?)

Aboard the MV *Columbia*, well away on our journey out of Alaska, a woman came across the aisle in the snack bar and stopped at our table. "You don't know me, but I wanted to tell you that we're going to miss you in Anchorage," she said.

I'd heard that a few times before departing; the people who were glad to see me go mainly had the good grace not to say so to my face. I smiled and told her I knew I was going to miss Alaska, too.

My wife first noticed the woman's husband — a trim seventy-year-old with a neat white goatee and a Levis jacket: Keith Miller, third governor of Alaska. They were en route back to their winter home in Florence, Oregon, after a summer in Girdwood.

"You'll be back," he told us.

And who am I to argue with that? 🜚

About the Editor

Mike Doogan, a lifelong Alaskan, is a columnist at the *Anchorage Daily News* where his subject matter covers the human terrain of Alaska ranging from humor to populist observations about politicians and bureaucrats.

Doogan refuses to take himself too seriously. He has won many awards for journalism, including a share of the Pulitzer Prize. But he knows how to have fun, having written two books filled with that special brand of Alaska humor, *HOW TO SPEAK ALASKAN* and *FASHION MEANS YOUR FUR HAT IS DEAD*, both published by Epicenter Press.

Doogan also teaches writing, having recently earned a master of fine arts degree in creative writing from the University of Alaska Anchorage. He and his wife, Kathy, have two grown children.

Recommendations for readers seeking a greater understanding of Alaska's people:

ARCTIC BUSH PILOT: A Memoir, by James "Andy" Anderson as told to Jim Rearden, trade paperback, $16.95.

ART & ESKIMO POWER: The Life & Times of Alaskan Howard Rock, by Lael Morgan, trade paperback, $16.95.

COLD RIVER SPIRITS: The Legacy of an Athabascan Irish-Family from Alaska's Yukon River, by Jan Harper-Haines, hardbound, $19.95.

COLD STARRY NIGHT: An Alaska Memoir, by Claire Fejes, trade paperback, $19.95.

FASHION MEANS YOUR FUR HAT IS DEAD: A Guide to Good Manners & Social Survival in Alaska, by Mike Doogan, trade paperback, $14.95.

FATHER OF THE IDITAROD: The Joe Redington Story, by Lew Freedman, trade paperback, $16.95.

MOMENTS RIGHTLY PLACED: An Aleutian Memoir, by Ray Hudson, trade paperback, $14.95.

RIDING THE WILD SIDE OF DENALI, by Miki & Julie Collins, trade paperback, $14.95.

TALES OF ALASKA'S BUSHRAT GOVERNOR: The Extraordinary Autobiography of Jay Hammond, Wilderness Guide and Reluctant Politician, trade paperback, $17.95.

These titles can be found or special-ordered at your local bookstore. A wide assortment of Alaska books also can be ordered at the publisher's website, EpicenterPress.com or by calling 800-950-6663 day or night.

EPICENTER PRESS
Alaska Book Adventures
www.EpicenterPress.com